1. 11

Cake Decorating for
All Seasons

Cake Decorating for All Seasons

A Step-by-Step Guide

Lucy Poulton

MEREHURST PRESS
LONDON

This edition published 1988
by Merehurst Press
5 Great James Street, London WC1N 3DA
by arrangement with Viking O'Neil

ISBN 1 85391 027 9

Produced by Viking O'Neil
56 Claremont Street, South Yarra, Victoria 3141, Australia
A division of Penguin Books Australia Ltd

Designed by Sandra Nobes
Illustrations by Lorraine Ellis
Photography by Mike Fisher
Typeset in Cheltenham by Bookset, North Melbourne, Victoria
Printed and bound in Hong Kong through Bookbuilders Limited

CONTENTS

INTRODUCTION

The theme of this book has been inspired by the desire to capture in sugar some of the beauty and colour of the four seasons. It also seemed particularly fitting to follow the seasons because, for most of us, the rich and changing tapestry of nature is intimately associated with the milestones and celebrations in our lives.

Traditionally cakes for special occasions have been decorated with flowers, yet so often the flowers selected have borne no relation to the season of the celebration. By exploring the flora of the different seasons, *Cake Decorating for All Seasons* redresses this shortcoming and offers a great range of possibilities for floral sprays and themes for floodwork.

Cake Decorating for All Seasons is arranged in four sections according to the seasons, the cakes within each reflecting the colours, flora and festivities of the particular time of the year. A chapter on basic techniques that are relevant to all cake decorating, such as covering the cake, precedes these sections. Instructions for all the detailed techniques of cake decorating, such as cocoa butter painting, floodwork, embroidery piping, writing, decoration moulding and extension work, are given throughout the book. Although obviously these techniques are not restricted to the cakes of any one season, each is discussed in detail in the seasonal section most appropriate to it. For example, because spring is the season best known for flowers, flower presentation is dealt with in the Spring section.

The ideas presented here should encourage you to create your own seasonal cakes, adapting the techniques and designs explained in the book to suit the celebrations of your year.

CONVERSION TABLES

Weights

Metric	Imperial
15 g	½ oz
30 g	1 oz
60 g	2 oz
90 g	3 oz
125 g	4 oz
185 g	6 oz
250 g	8 oz
500 g	16 oz (1 lb)
1000 g (1 kg)	32 oz (2 lb)

Liquid Measures

Metric	Imperial	Household measure
5 ml	—	1 teaspoon
15 ml	½ fl oz	—
30 ml	1 fl oz	1 tablespoon
60 ml	3 fl oz	—
150 ml	5 fl oz	—
250 ml	8 fl oz	1 cup
600 ml	20 fl oz	1 pint

Cake Tin Sizes

Metric	Imperial
15 cm	6 inches
17 cm	7 inches
20 cm	8 inches
22 cm	9 inches
25 cm	10 inches
30 cm	12 inches

Oven Temperature Guide

	Electric		Gas	
	°C	°F	°C	°F
Low or cool	95	200	95	200
Very slow	120	250	120	250
Slow or warm	150	300	150–160	300–325
Moderately slow	160	325	160–175	325–350
Moderate	175	350	175–190	350–375
Moderately hot	190	375	190–205	375–400
Hot	205	400	205–230	400–450
Very hot	230	450	230–260	450–500

BASIC TECHNIQUES

Equipment

The large variety of cake decorating equipment available today can make this hobby quite expensive. This is especially so if you mistakenly believe that all the equipment must be acquired before a beautiful cake can be produced. All the items listed below have been included because they were used to produce the decorations described in this book. There are many others which have not been included because they are not relevant to the work described or because substitutes can be used. A large number of household items can be adapted to your needs which reduces storage problems as well as cost. Remember that it is not always the most expensive equipment which produces the best results. Experiment and adapt items to your needs. Such items can lend a personalised style to the articles produced.

Icing Tubes

Use numbers 00, 0, 1 and 3 for writing or any line work and star tubes numbers 5 and 8. Use a suitably cut paper cone or bag instead of a leaf tube.

Parchmentene Paper

This is available from cake decorating and specialty stores. Greaseproof paper, non-stick baking paper, tracing paper and vegetable parchment paper are all suitable substitutes for making piping bags or cones. These allow more control and less wastage than the cloth or plastic alternatives.

Colours

A wide selection of liquid, paste and powder colours is available. These are discussed in detail on pp. 11–14.

Eye Dropper

Any medicinal dropper is suitable, especially if it has measurement markings. Use it for liquid colours.

Paint Brushes

A variety of paint brushes will enhance your colouring techniques. Fine hair such as sable or ox is the best for very light, fine colour work. There are now many synthetic bristles which are also very good so, if cost is a problem, these can be used as an alternative. Hog hair is strong and much firmer but it is only recommended for some cocoa painting work. Brush sizes will vary from brand to brand so use the following only as a guide: numbers 00, 0, 3, 5 and 8 for sable hair brushes; flat sable or hog hair brushes in 5 mm and 1 cm widths; hog hair brushes, round or flat, in numbers 0, 1, 2 and 3. These should be purchased from an artists' supply store since most cake decorating stores do not carry a very good range.

Scissors

A large pair is needed for cutting wire and ribbons. A small, fine, straight-bladed pair, such as those used for embroidery, is essential to achieve pretty and delicate moulded flowers.

Tweezers

You need either a short or long handled pair to use for placing stamens, ribbons and flowers in arrangements. Flat, straight ends are better than the pointed variety.

Cutters

These are very useful when producing moulded flowers. However, it can be quite costly to purchase each cutter referred to in all the flower-making instructions in this book. An economical approach to this problem is to purchase a small collection and then make the remainder as required. You need to buy the very small daphne and forget-me-not cutters which cannot be made at home because they are made on a last. The frangipani, rose and waterlily cutters are used extensively because they can also be adapted to make many other flowers. This adaptability, combined with their durability, makes it advisable to buy these also. All other cutters can be made as required.

Strip Metal

Metal strips cut to an appropriate length and width can be shaped over a template to make any number of cutters. Once the metal has been shaped to the required design, use a stapler to hold the ends together and then trim away any excess metal. Fold and turn the stapled end so that it is flat against the side of the cutter. A little practice will be required for this work but once perfected it will prove not only economical, but also very versatile. In this way flowers and leaves can be tailor-made and you are not limited to the size and shape of cutters which are mass produced. Suitable metals for this work are shim brass or copper, or thin strips of aluminium flashing. These are available from hardware or plumbing suppliers. Two other alternatives are available: cut empty soft drink cans into strips by using a strong, sharp pair of scissors or use the layer of foil from the top of tins of coffee to make up strips.

Moulding Tools

Although there are now many moulding tools especially made for cake decorating, they are not always known by the same names. Many kits actually include pottery tools, all of which are not necessarily required, so it is best to purchase items according to your individual needs. The following items will be useful although the list is only a guide. A long-handled pin or needle is useful for marking patterns and inserting ribbons and flowers into sprays. A rounded tool, either curved or in the shape of a ball, can be used for 'balling' petals. A small and a large balling tool are useful although, for very small work, the rounded end of a curler pin is most effective. A veining tool is used to mark in veins on leaves; any long, narrow, flat-edged tool is suitable. A hollowing tool is also useful. It is a round, pointed tool, shaped like a round arrow head either smooth or ridged. The ridged version can make internal indentations.

Cocktail Sticks

These are used to help frill and flute paste or icing.

Alternatives are bamboo skewers or butchers' wooden skewers which have been sanded down to the required shape.

Thin Rubber

A small piece of thin rubber is invaluable for working petals or flowers. If thinning and fluting is required the rubber allows the paste to be worked with less chance of it tearing.

Stamens

Although a wide range of stamens is available from cake decorating suppliers, small white-tipped stamens are the most versatile. These can be enlarged with paste and coloured with food colours.

Cotton-covered Wire

Fine-gauge wire is the most frequently used. However, medium and thick are also very useful. A nylon or silk-covered wire is now available for extra fine work. There is also a paper-covered wire available in various thicknesses. Although these wires are available in green, white or cream, it is best to purchase white and then colour according to need.

Working Board

A small, compact working surface is required for rolling out paste. A smooth, shiny bathroom tile is ideal for this since it has a stain-free, washable surface. Use a dark-coloured tile for better contrast especially if you are going to practise piping work on it.

Rolling Pin

A large pin about 500 mm long is required for rolling out large amounts of icing. The extra length enables the icing to be lifted onto the cake without leaving marks made from the edges. A small, thinner pin of about 150 mm gives better control when rolling out small quantities of paste for making up flowers and ornaments.

Extras

The following items are very useful but not essential: ruler and tape measure; wooden spoons; extra-fine sieves; turntable, either flat or tilting; patty tin; foam; foil; waxed paper; and a piece of florist's oasis for drying flowers.

Colours and Colouring Techniques

Colouring is by far the most important part of cake decorating. Fine, dainty flowers can be destroyed by harsh colours while cakes covered in vibrantly coloured icing do absolutely nothing for the appetite. When selecting a colour scheme consideration should be given to the following points.

□ There should be a balance between the shape and size of your cake and its decorations. These should be in graded sizes with deep or bright colours presented in a balanced range so that the cake is not dwarfed.

□ Although in nature many flowers are brilliant, care should be taken when reproducing these for a cake. Petals on real flowers are often translucent or even transparent so that a red flower will not look harsh because of the sun's highlights. A sugar flower will look stiff and unreal if it is tinted in the same tones. To overcome this problem, check individual petals to establish what range of tones can be found within them. Use a variety of colours to make up your colour. If there are no highlights, make up your own because you have to reproduce the interplay of light and colour on each petal. Some areas of the flower can be left almost white so as to give this effect.

□ Become more observant and conscious of detail. Does a picture have details which you have not noticed? What are the various tones of a colour? Consider the colour red: if it is a cool red it may have blue, grey or green within it.

□ Many flowers and leaves have traces of other colours within them. This smudging of colour gives a 'bleeding' effect. An ideal flower for this study is the fuchsia. The base of the flower may have traces of green as if the stem and leaves have smudged their colour onto the base, or even onto the tip of some petals. In the case of red fuchsias the stems and many of the younger leaves have traces of red. The pink honeysuckle is another example, with many of the leaves on this plant having dark pink veins and stems. Some very pale pink roses have a slight tinge of white-green at the centre base of their petals. Learn to use this bleeding effect to advantage on your work, because this will ensure it looks realistic.

□ Use a colour wheel to get best results from your colour combinations. Colours opposite each other make the best contrasts while colours beside each other give you good colour gradings.

□ Make up a colour chart to assist you. Use a collection of colours, a series of water-filled jars, a brush and a large piece of blotting paper. Add one drop of colour to the water then add another drop of a different colour. Brush a little of the water onto the paper and then write the details underneath. For example, one drop of blue plus one drop of red produces purple. More red gives a maroon purple while more blue gives a violet shade. If an extensive chart is made you will always have a reference to guide your colouring.

□ Colours are available in several forms and some are more suitable for certain effects. Petal dust is ideal for a soft, hazy appearance. Liquid colours are best for large areas. Paste colours are less messy and are therefore ideal for colouring fondant icing or paste. Combinations of all, or some varieties, will assist when it is difficult to achieve the tone required. An example of this is red. If red is required within a piece of floodwork, or for a red rose, there are various alternatives. The colour can be added to the icing or paste and then, when the item is completely dry, it can be brushed over with a powder to intensify the tone. Tinges of other colours can also be added to make the red appear more lifelike.

□ Note that non-toxic pastels are not food colours and so should be used with caution. Do not eat items coloured with pastels. It is wise to replace pastel colours with petal dust wherever possible.

□ It is better to understate colours even when dealing with dark or bright-coloured items. A softer version of the real thing may look far more realistic than a completely true replica.

Once all these factors have been taken into account there is still the task of actually colouring cakes, flowers or floodwork. This colouring creates problems for many decorators, regardless of experience. Since it is impossible to give individual details for every flower (there are also many variations between plants of the same species), the following suggestions are offered as a guide. Remember that many varieties of flowers have similar colours and can therefore be tinted in the same way.

Before commencing on suggested colouring methods it is best to be aware of the variety of available colours.

Petal Dusts

These are very fine powdered colours which have a cornflour base. They are available in a variety of shades and can be mixed to achieve a wider range of colours. If lighter tones are required, the dusts can be mixed with a little cornflour. They can be used dry or moistened with water or spirits. Petal dusts are also available in a frosted range which can be used to create a glitter effect on particular decorations. These colours are not available at all supply stores.

Powder Colours

If petal dust is not available, experiment with powder colours. These come in a wide variety of shades. They are true food colours, so they can be very strong. Be careful not to stain cakes or equipment accidentally. Powder colours are ideal for those occasions when dark colours are required. If a softer tone is preferred, add a small quantity of powder to some cornflour and test for strength. If liquid colour is required, this can be made by dissolving the powder in a little hot water. Store any remaining colour in a small bottle.

Non-toxic Chalk Pastels

Although not strictly food colours, chalk-like pastels are now used by many decorators to achieve a greater colour range in their work. They can be used in the same way as the dusts but they are not as fine or as safe. Oil pastels cannot be used. The chalk pastels are scraped or worked onto paper, producing a fine powder which is collected and applied, either as a dry dust or as a moistened liquid. For dry applications, use a dry brush and apply directly to the required surface. Lighten colours with cornflour if paler shades are needed. When this powder is moistened, ensure that all particles are completely dissolved before using. This will eliminate dark, streaky patches. Because these pastels are not food products – though they are non-toxic – it is advisable to use them with caution if the coloured areas are to be eaten.

Liquid Colours

Liquid food colours are stronger than, and different from, coloured food flavours. They have a water base, so they can also be diluted with water. Note, however, that when very pale shades are required it is best to use methylated spirits instead of water. This is used so that the sugar will not dissolve. This method allows the colour to remain while the spirit evaporates. Unfortunately the additives in the spirits leave a bitter taste but this can be reduced by using either surgical or pure spirits.

Paste Colours

These are very clean and excellent for colouring a large amount of fondant icing. They are very economical but some may not be true to colour, so test before using these. Most paste colours are edible. Some that are oil based can also be used for colouring chocolate. Take a ball of icing (or paste) about the size of a golf ball, and knead the colour in to mix it evenly. If the result appears to be a good, darker tone of the required colour, knead the ball into the larger mass of icing. If it seems too dark, only add a portion of the coloured ball.

Flowers with a Tinge of Colour

Many flowers are described as white flowers. In fact, when flowers are studied more closely, there are not many which are just plain white with no other colour. Flowers such as honeysuckle, white lobelia, chrysanthemum, camellia, primula, rhododendron, violet, waxflower, the broom known as bridal veil, clematis and coastal rosemary are all white with a tinge of colour. These tinges can be green, pink, violet, lemon or gold, and they can vary from being a small area of spots to a hazy blur of colour either on the petals or on the underside of the flower.

Flowers which have colouring on the underside should have just a slight tinge of colour brushed on the base of the flowers. Inspect the real thing and then reproduce the effect on the sugar ones. If the colour fades from the base up, allow a minimum of petal dust and brush the colour on with an upward motion. It does not matter what colour is used as the technique remains the same.

Deeper tones in the throat of a flower can be achieved in the opposite way. Brush a little colour at the base on the inside of the flower and draw the brush strokes up to get a faded, soft effect as the flower opens. Once again petal dust is best for this sort of work.

Haze and spots can also be found together on such flowers as rhododendrons and the whiter coastal rosemary. For this purpose it is best to brush a soft haze of colour on the relevant petals, making sure that you take note of how far the colour extends. To paint the spots, return with a moistened brush with just a little colour, and paint on a mass of soft, hazy spots. Wipe any excess colour onto a dry cloth before each application and place the spots in a series of small dabs rather than heavy circular dots. If there are to be many spots it may be helpful to brush the petal with a small amount of clear methylated spirits and then return to paint the spots when the petals are partially dry. This will assist the bleeding effect and give the spots a softer appearance.

Shading

This technique can be used for flowers which have a range of colours. The tones may all be of the same colour or you can combine shaded variations of two or more colours. Flowers which require this technique include bougainvillea, fan-flower, morning glory, running postman, waterlily, chrysanthemum, cineraria, camellia, happy wanderer, wisteria and periwinkle.

Colour all the relevant areas in the lightest tone first. Return and re-colour the areas which need the middle tones and then finally colour the darkest parts with a third application. Allow some bleeding between the various shades so they appear more natural. Areas which are to be white can have just the slightest hint of a very pale shade of the colour. In some flowers, the white may be tinged with lemon or green so the tingeing method can be used for this effect. If any of these petals have a hint of another colour, be sure to include a little of this colour before commencing. For example, if a mauve colour has a hint of lemon, the lemon should be included before any colouring has commenced.

Dark-edged Petals

Many flowers require this highlight effect. Once the flower has been coloured, run a slightly moist brush along the edge of the petal's thickness. Slightly moisten the flower with methylated spirits to assist this. The colour will bleed into the paste resulting in a darker and shaded tone on the edge. Care must be taken not to use too much liquid because the harsh tone will destroy the effect.

Final Flower Colouring

Stamens and stigmas are the final parts of the flower to be coloured. Use the same colours as those used for the flowers – or darker shades if you wish. You may need to colour only the tips and possibly the cotton length as well. Methylated spirits will be required for this painting because water is not suitable.

Stamens and wires can be coloured by either painting with coloured methylated spirits or dipping. Wire and ribbon can be coloured by placing them in a jar containing coloured methylated spirits. Remove and pat dry between paper towels and then, when dry, test for colour. If darker shades are required the item may be returned for a second or third treatment. Stamens cannot be recoloured in this way because the waxed cottons will become soft and limp.

Any coloured flowers can be touched up with a combination of various colours. Brush a little grey or pale blue dry dust onto the flowers for colours which are too stark. Red dry powder in conjunction with yellow may improve an otherwise lifeless flower. Eucalyptus leaves and gumnuts are much improved with the addition of a layer of grey or black powder. If a grainy effect is required, powdered pastel can be used on items which have been moistened with methylated spirits. This will allow the grains to adhere but not dissolve.

Spray Colouring

Flowers can also be coloured using a spray method. This technique is very useful when large numbers are to be coloured. Use a very fine spray nozzle for this work so that colours remain soft and delicate. The old style hairdressers' lacquer spray bottles are best.

Two or three different colours can be sprayed to create a variety of effects. This technique is especially useful when treating flowers which require two-tone effects. A good example of this is the bougainvillea; seen under dull light the flower seems to be purple while in brighter conditions it appears to have a pink tinge. Spray pink onto the flower as a base tone and then spray it with purple before the first colour dries.

Cakes and Cake Covering

Fruit cake is the traditional cake used for decorating. There are many other firm cakes which can be successfully decorated but fruit cakes are usually used because they do not spoil during the time required for decorating. Fruit cakes actually improve in flavour while they mature and this is an added bonus for the decorator. Check the recipe section in this book for a selection of suitable cakes.

Cake Tins

Cake decorating equipment can be expensive. There is a wide range of cake tins available so shop around before you buy. Cake tins are available from department and specialty stores.

For single tier cakes everyday tins can be used. If the cake is to be a particularly large one, baking tins can be converted for this use. If your cake is to be baked in a microwave oven your needs will be different. If tiered cakes are to be made then best results are achieved by using a set of matching tins. These are usually hand-made so they will be much dearer than the mass produced ones. Remember that the more intricate the shape, the more expensive the tin is likely to be. It is possible to hire cake tins from some stores. Problems can arise when using an assortment of different tins. Look for uniformity of height as well as of corners or outer edges. This will save many hours of work, and the cost of extra icing required for packing the corners if the tins do not match.

If a very large tin is to be used, measure your oven before making your purchase, to make sure that it will fit. If you want a large cake, two smaller square or rectangular cakes can be joined together to make a larger size, or a ready-made cake can be purchased from a bakery.

Cake Sizes

When calculating the volume of cake mixture required for your tin, fill an 8 in or 20 cm tin with water to 2–3 cm from the top of the tin. Pour this water into a measuring jug and note the volume. The 20 cm tin holds one quantity of a 500 g butter recipe, so make your calculations accordingly. As a final consideration, take into account the fact that cakes which are to form tiers should be the same height, so keep this in mind when filling the tins. It is possible to have your cakes diminishing in height if you are concerned about cost. The bottom tier should be the highest with the others reducing by 1 cm per cake.

Cake size requirements are calculated on the basis that an 8 in or 20 cm cake will cater for eighty guests. This will allow a small thin slice per person, so if more generous serves are required this should be taken into consideration. Remember that a small, decorated cake may be sufficient if a second iced but undecorated cake is provided for extra cutting.

Cake Shapes

The large range of cake tins now available makes it possible to produce cakes in many shapes and sizes. There are the traditional round and square shapes, and some other ornate fancy shapes such as the petal and the horseshoe. If, however, something a little different is required, it is possible to utilise household items to create unusual forms.

Ball Cakes

Two pudding bowls can be used to produce a ball-shaped cake. Bake two cakes and then trim any peak which has formed on the top. Insert three wooden skewers into the flat surface of one cake so that the top half of each skewer is still visible. Glaze the flat surface of the other cake with hot jam and then invert it onto the first. Push down gently so that the skewers are lodged firmly into the second cake. Note that the skewers should not protrude past the outer edge of the cakes. If there are any small gaps between the two cakes, these can be filled with a little almond icing.

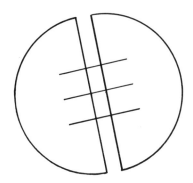

Cylindrical Cakes

This shape is ideal for cakes which are to be presented as candles, columns or tall vases. Although

tins such as those for making nut loaves are suitable, they are often too small. Tins from preserved fruits, biscuits or coffee can be used. Do not overfill these tins because, if the mixture rises a little, the contents may spill over the top. If a very tall cake is required, bake two cakes and then attach them in the same way as the ball cakes above.

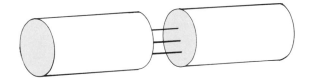

Freestyle Cakes

Unusual, asymmetrical shapes can be made by moulding firm foil which can be kept in shape by sewing or stapling the seams. If no heavy duty sheets of foil are available, foil baking trays may be used. Use the rounded end of a rolling pin to press out the original shape and then mould the piece into the required shape. Staple several pieces together if a larger cake is required, then mould into shape. Cakes representing driftwood or shells can be made in this way as well as novelty animal cakes. Photographs or samples of the real thing can be of great assistance. Remember that your cake is to be baked in the improvised shape, so make sure the base is flat enough to provide stability. Otherwise the cake mixture will spill out.

Adapted Shapes

Traditional shapes can also be altered to make something just a little different. The top of a cake can be trimmed to make a slant or a curve or small sections can be cut away to allow for a hollow in which to place your spray of ornaments. Corners can be cut for a completely different shape. A pliable metal insert can be placed in the tin prior to filling with cake mixture to produce a new shape. Experiment with these ideas to produce new and original shapes for your cakes.

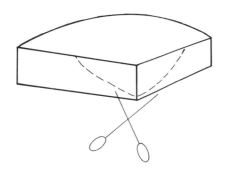

Preparation for Covering

Freestyle cakes are particularly fragile so allow them to rest for a week before commencing any decorating work. Patch and fill any holes with almond icing. Use pieces of icing to pack any areas which are not quite symmetrical. If there are any parts of the cake which appear too fragile for handling, strengthen these by inserting bamboo or wooden skewers into the cake. Allow this patching to dry for several days before commencing the almond covering.

Although care must be taken with the final covering of these cakes, it is not such a difficult task to achieve a nice, smooth finish. Soft icing is very pliable so it can be rolled out and applied in the usual way. When smoothing out this covering, allow the icing to be moulded into the curves and hollows which have been made. Very flexible, small cake scrapers should be used instead of the traditional larger ones. The smaller scrapers can be made by cutting small rectangles from pliable plastic. Empty ice-cream containers are good for this purpose.

Cake Tin Preparations

There is much debate about whether or not cake tins should be lined. The decision is usually a matter of personal choice, but the size and shape of your cake needs to be taken into account. It may not be possible to line the tin for some of the more unusual cakes. Foil shapes, for instance, do not lend themselves to lining. Baking times should also be taken into account. For instance, cake tins larger than 8 in or 20 cm in diameter should be lined. As the baking time can be six or more hours, a lining will reduce the possibility of burning. If you prefer not to line these tins it is possible to

reduce the drying out process by wrapping moistened sheets of newspaper around the outside of the tin. Allow an extra half-hour cooking time when using this method.

One or two layers of brown paper and two or three layers of greaseproof paper should be used for lining. The thickness should be determined by the size of the cake. The larger the cake, the thicker the lining. If a very thick brown paper is used only one layer is necessary.

All linings should be as smooth as possible because if there are any creases these will be baked into the cake surface. Do not use salted butter for greasing your paper and tins because the salt will induce burning over a lengthy baking period. Use either unsalted butter or a good quality vegetable oil. To help avoid creases, grease each layer of lining as well as the tin so that the sheets of paper adhere to each other.

Since the cakes swell during baking, linings should not be constricting. Allow a 2–3 cm overlap at corners and seams so that the lining can spread as the cake swells. A tight, restricting lining will result in a cake which appears to be wider at the base than the top.

Round and Fancy Tins

Round, oval and fancy cake tins require a base lining and two, three or more side pieces. The number of side-lining pieces is determined by the size of the cake: the larger the cake the greater the number of pieces. The side pieces should be cut 6 cm higher than the height of the tin so that 3 cm can be used under the base lining, leaving the other 3 cm above the height of the tin. Side pieces should overlap each other by 3–5 cm so that they will spread out during baking. To enable the base 3 cm of these side pieces to be tucked in under the base lining, make a fold at the 3 cm point of each piece. Make a series of cuts 2–3 cm apart along the length of each piece, in towards the fold. The small cut pieces so formed can then be overlapped on

This diamond cake has a slanted top to accentuate its shape and to make it easier to see the picture painted in cocoa butter. This unusual method of presentation also highlights the extensiveness of the painted landscape and adds to the three-dimensional effect. The sugar grasses complement the golds and browns of a dry, hot summer. (Instructions: Cake Shapes, p. 15; Cocoa Butter Painting, p. 23; Grasses, p. 41.)

16

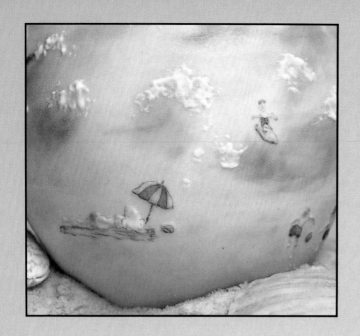

the base of the tin. They can be fitted snugly around any curves and pressed in evenly at the corners. Insert the base lining once all the side pieces are in place.

Square and other angular-shaped tins can be lined in the same way as described above or covered with single pieces cut appropriately. Measure the base width and length of the cake and then include twice the height of the side plus an extra 6 cm. Cut your paper accordingly. Place the tin in the centre of the paper and mark out the base. Remove the tin and crease the paper along these base lines. Following the illustration below, make cuts in the paper along the dotted lines. Work from left to right until all the corners have been done. Cut away small rectangles so that, when the lining is placed in the tin, the overlap at each corner will not be more than 3–5 cm. Crease firm corners into the paper once it is in place to assist the overall shape.

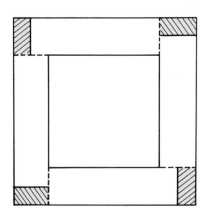

Note that drips of butter or mixture can escape during baking so place cake tins on a flat baking tray to catch these.

Baking Hints

☐ After filling your cake tin with mixture, drop it from a height to allow all the air bubbles to escape.

A ball-shaped cake highlights the carefree mood of summer. The beach games decorating the surface have been done in floodwork. The sand is coloured sugar which has been sprayed with a fine film of water to help keep it in place. The beach shells on the sand are also made from sugar. (Instructions: Ball Cakes, p. 15; Shells, p. 29; Floodwork, p. 54; Floodwork Colouring, p. 55.)

☐ Smooth the top of the cake by running a moistened tablespoon over the surface. Repeat this until a thin layer of water forms on the top of the cake. This will ensure a smooth and even finish.

☐ Make one or more small dips in the centre of the cake. This prevents the cake rising to a peak. Longer cakes such as the large rectangles may require a number of dips in a line along the centre of the cake.

☐ Place a piece of foil or brown paper over the top of the cake during baking. The cake will still brown but it will remain moist. The moisture will evaporate and condense on the inside of the foil and then be returned to the cake. This will continue during baking and cooling so that as much moisture as possible can be retained within the cake.

☐ Remove the cake from the oven once it is cooked. Do not remove the foil. Cover the cake with a blanket or something similar and leave for 24 hours. Do not leave the cake in the oven to cool because this dries it out.

☐ You can remove the cake from the oven just a little before it is ready. Latent heat will continue cooking it. This reduces the risk of burning and drying out.

☐ If cake tins are not lined they can be greased and then sprinkled with flour before filling. Cake tins that are lined do not require very much greasing if the linings have been greased.

☐ Cakes can be baked up to 24 hours after they have been mixed. Make up the mixture in the usual way, place it in the tin and then put the tin in the refrigerator until ready to bake.

☐ If there is no cream of tartar in the flour, a cake mixture can be made up and frozen until ready to bake. The cake can be baked either from its pre-cooked frozen state or thawed out and then cooked. Allow extra cooking time for frozen cake mixtures.

Cake Boards

Cake boards are traditionally covered either in silver or gold quality foil. This foil is not the same as that used for baking. One side is metallic while the back has a paper surface. Foils are available in colours as well as gold or silver, and at Christmas there are also multi-toned patterned foils. Most plain foils have embossed patterns. It is important to ensure that tiered cakes are presented on matching covered boards.

Boards should be chosen according to the size and weight of a cake. Tiered cakes require sets of boards which are the same shape. If you want a more unusual presentation it may be necessary to place the cakes on individual boards and then set them onto a larger one. It is also possible to present cakes on boards covered with velvet or wood-grain contact depending upon the chosen theme. Cakes can also be placed on mirrored glass, but need to be removed from the glass before they are cut.

Very thick, sturdy cardboard is available for cake boards but be sure it is strong enough to support the weight of the cake. Boards can be purchased ready cut and covered or they can be cut according to your own needs.

When making a tiered cake, the boards will vary in width and thickness. The base board needs to support the weight of all the cakes so this should be a little thicker than the others. Use a chipboard of up to 1.5 cm thickness for this. The base board can be much larger than the cake. This may be desirable so that decorations can be presented to best advantage. It will also reduce the risk of breakages if side designs are elaborate or fragile. Other boards of tiered cakes can be much smaller although they should be larger than the cakes they are supporting. The boards can be from 3–10 cm larger than the cake, depending on the final effect you want.

Fancy tiered cakes can be presented on matching shaped boards or square, rectangular or round boards depending on choice. If a plainer board is used for the base cake you may wish to use a fancy cut board for other cakes in the tier to reduce shadows.

Covering the Boards

To cover the boards, cut your paper large enough to allow a 4–6 cm rim on the underside. Spread some good quality glue or paste all over the underside of the paper and then place the board in the centre. If the paste does not have much strength, it may be necessary to spread some on the board also. Press down firmly so that the paper is attached securely. If the board is fancy or round make a series of small cuts along the outer rim in the same way as prescribed for the lining of Round and Fancy Tins (see p. 16). Press the cut sections down one by one allowing them to overlap where necessary so that a nice, clean finish is achieved.

Be sure to press firmly along the edge of the board so that the paper sits snugly against the board. Remove any air bubbles by pricking the bubble and then smoothing down with the fingers. Cornered cake boards do not require the series of cuts on the underside. Just cut away small sections at the corners so that, when the paper is folded, it covers the board leaving a nice, smooth corner.

Cover the underside of the board with a piece of the same paper or with some plain white paper, smaller than the board. When the covered board is completely dry the cake may be placed on it.

Board Runners

Single tier and base boards should have small runners on the underside. Without these it is sometimes very difficult to lift the cake. Runners should not be too high or uneven in height. For a quick and easy runner, glue three or four wooden curtain rings onto the base of a covered board. Always ensure these runners are neat because they will detract from the appearance of the cake if they are visible.

Covering Cakes

Method

1 Before you begin covering it is necessary to fill in any small holes which are visible on the surface of the cake. Knead a small amount of icing between the fingers and then push it into the holes. Press and smooth the icing by using a small, flat spatula or a blunt knife. Continue in this way until all the holes have been filled. Any other holes, bumps or spaces should also be filled before covering. If there are ridges or spaces at the top or base of a cake, these should be filled at this time.

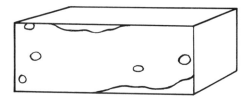

Regardless of whether the top or bottom is to be used as the upper surface of the decorated cake, some patching and filling will usually have to be done. If a peak or depressed ridge has formed, this will have to be removed. Roll out sausage-shaped pieces of icing and press them into the vacant areas. If a peak is very high but the cake height is low, it may be necessary to cut away only a part of the peak and pack the remainder to give some extra height. Use a firm pair of scrapers to press the icing into the spaces and to retain the cake's shape.

If it has been necessary to wedge a lot of icing into the spaces at the base of the cake, leave it to dry for a week or two before moving the cake to another board. Cakes can be iced on a working board or on the presentation board. Allow at least two weeks drying if the cake is to be moved once it has been covered. To lift the cake, loosen it from the board by running a knife under the base. Place strong cake lifters under the left and right of the cake. Lift the cake and rest it on the new board. Before removing the lifters place a scraper against the side of the cake, above where the lifter is located. Hold this firmly against the cake as the lifter is drawn away. Repeat for the other side. This will reduce the risk of damage to the icing.

Note that for the best results, allow patches to dry for two or three days before covering with almond icing. Otherwise patches may pop out a little during the covering, giving a rippled appearance to the almond surface.

Fruit cakes are normally covered with two layers of icing: the first is usually almond icing; the second is known as soft icing. The almond icing not only gives the cake a rich flavour but it also ensures that fruit staining does not occur on the final covering. The natural oils contained within this icing act as a barrier to stop the covering from becoming yellow and discoloured as a result of contact with the fruits. If a cake is to be used within two to three weeks, this almond layer can be omitted. If a single layer of icing is to be used, it should be 1–2 cm thick. If you find the almond taste too strong, the first covering can be a 50:50 mixture of almond and soft icing or even a 30:70 combination. Knead the two icings very well before applying to the cake.

An average 8 inch or 20 cm cake requires 1 kg of almond icing for the first covering. Knead the icing a little to ensure it is smooth and pliable. Once it is ready to use, roll it into a ball with all the creases and lines on the underside. Shape the ball according to the shape of the cake and then begin to roll it out.

It is commonly stated that icings should be rolled out on a bed of pure icing sugar. This is considered to be the only sure way to avoid fermentation occurring once the icing has been placed on the cake. However, icing sugar can be a little grainy and it is possible to use cornflour instead. If desired, the almond icing can be rolled on icing sugar and the outer icing rolled on cornflour. The final choice in this matter is a personal one.

2   Roll out the icing using a very long rolling pin to ensure that no lines are indented by the outer edge of the pin. A long piece of PVC piping makes an ideal stain-free rolling pin. Measure your cake by running a tape measure from the base on one side, across the top and down the other side. Your icing should be rolled out to this exact measurement. If your icing is too large it becomes difficult to handle and if it is too small it may tear when stretched.

3   Before covering your cake glaze it all over. Use any variety of seedless jam or a combination of glucose and spirits. Heat the ingredients until they come to the boil and then use a pastry brush to glaze a thin covering all over the cake. If the mixture seems too thick, add a little water during heating.

4   Place the rolling pin across the top part of the icing. This is the part furthest from the body. Roll about half of the icing onto the pin using a forward motion. Lift the pin with the icing and then hold it over the top of the cake so that the icing will fall evenly on each side of the cake. Allow the base part of the unrolled icing to just touch the base of the cake board. This is the part closest to the body. Draw the rolling pin away from the body and, at the same time, unroll the icing from the pin and onto the cake. It should roll over the cake and across to the back. Gently roll the top a little to ensure the icing becomes attached.

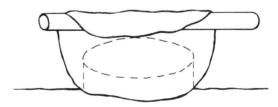

5   Gently press around the rim of the cake with your hand. This will help ease the icing onto the surface. If there are creases and folds against the side of the cake do not press these against the cake; this will result in a pleated look. Regardless of shape, gently lift the icing with the left hand and press gently against the side with the right hand. Continue in this way until all the sides have been covered. If the icing is just pulled down the sides without allowing for this lifting, tears are inevitable. This process is meant to ease any folds down and away from the cake as well as reduce the possibility of tears. The folds and ripples will gradually be eased onto the excess icing which is on the board. Note that in the case of high cakes, this process may need to be repeated as you work around the cake. When the excess icing is trimmed there will be no creases or folds on the cake.

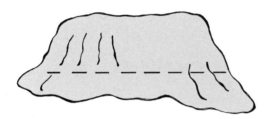

6 The excess icing should be trimmed slowly in order to avoid a short or fat look. Use either the base of a sharp scraper or a sharp knife to cut away all but 2 cm of the excess icing. Once this has been done, ease the icing against the sides of the cake by pushing gently against the base and the board.

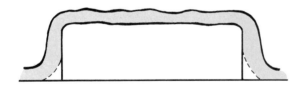

7 Return with the scraper and trim the remainder of the icing. This is done in small sections so that the icing can be pressed and eased against the side of the cake. The air will be removed and the icing allowed to fit snugly against the cake. Continue to work in this way until finished. During this process, note that if too much excess icing remains at the base, the cake will take on a waisted appearance, while if too much is removed the icing will look as if it has been cut short. Once completed, use two scrapers, one on either side of the cake, and work

all around the sides ensuring that the surface is smoothed and pressed firmly. Pinprick any air bubbles and press with the fingers to expel the air. Roll the top again and press with the scrapers. Then set the cake aside to dry.

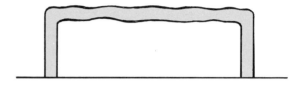

Final Covering

The final covering for a fruit cake is known as soft icing, fondant, plastic or sugar-paste. The different names are given by the various manufacturers but the product is the same. It is a pliable icing which is rolled and then placed on the cake. Although available in colours as well as white, it is advisable to colour your own icing to achieve very soft, pale tones.

Colouring Soft Icing

Take a small ball of icing and knead in three drops of liquid food colour or a very small amount of paste colour. When the colour appears to be well mixed, cut the ball in half to check for even distribution. If the cut surface is smooth and even in colour it is ready. If it is streaky, knead a little longer. If the coloured piece appears to be a dark tone of the required colour, the ball can be kneaded into the remainder of the icing. If it appears too dark or too light, adjust the tone. A lighter shade can be achieved by using only half the coloured ball while darker shades will require the addition of extra colour. Three drops of colour are usually adequate for colouring 1 kg of icing. The result will be a soft pale pastel tone. After the larger volume of icing has been coloured, test for even colouring by using the cutting test as above.

Covering with Soft Icing

Method

1 Roll out the icing as you did for the first covering (see Covering Cakes, step 2, p. 19). Do not wear any woollen clothing or anything which is dark in colour. These clothes release small fibres which may lodge in the icing. Remove all rings so they do not mark the final icing.

2 Once the icing has been rolled to the required size and shape, quickly brush the cake with another glaze. This can be boiling water, egg white or spirits. The icing can then be placed on the cake in the same way as the almond icing (see Covering Cakes, step 4, p. 19). Be careful not to stretch and tear the icing. Do not use too much icing sugar or cornflour when this icing is rolled out because it may cause fine hairline cracks to appear.

Overlay Covering

When a more unusual effect is required a cake can be covered in the normal way with the two layers of icing, allowed to dry and then an overlay covering applied. This overlay is a partial covering which allows some of the soft icing to remain visible. It is useful when two-tone icings are required or for enhancing fine, embroidered edges.

Method

1 Cover your cake in the normal way using first an almond covering and then a soft icing. Note that if two colours are to be used, the first soft icing should be coloured. Beautiful effects can be achieved by using two tones of the one colour. For example, if the colour of the first soft icing is pink, the overlay can be a lighter shade. Allow the cake to dry thoroughly for about two weeks before applying the second covering.

2 Colour the icing as required and then set this aside. Use a long strip of greaseproof paper to make up a pattern. This paper should be as long as the circumference and as high as the cake. Decide what the pattern is to be so that it can be drawn on the paper. An example of this would be a series of scallops falling down the sides of the cake. These can be shallow or deep depending on personal choice. Fold the paper according to the number of scallops needed and then draw one scallop from fold to fold. Cut the paper along the scallop line and unfold the paper so that a series of scallops is formed. Make up a second scalloped pattern in the same way.

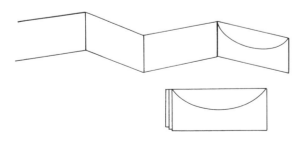

3 Place the paper around the base of the cake and use some sticky tape to hold the joins together. Use the end of a fine needle to lightly mark a line on the cake along all of these scallops. Be sure not to make any holes in the covering. Leave the paper in place during the second covering.

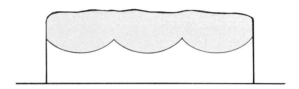

4 Measure the diameter of the cake and add twice the depth of the scallops. Roll out the icing to this length exactly. Using boiling water, egg white or spirits, glaze the parts of the cake which will be covered. Pick up the rolled icing in the same way as prescribed for covering (see Covering Cakes, step 4, p. 19) and then place it on the cake. Ensure the first edge only just touches the base of the scallops. Smooth the top and sides of the icing in the same way as for covering (see Covering Cakes, steps 5–7, p. 19).

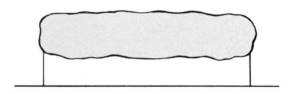

5 Place the second strip of scalloped paper on the base of the cake, and then use a small sharp knife to cut out the scallops at the base of the second covering. Because the first paper pattern is still in place, the second layer of icing will only adhere to the required areas so it will not be a problem to cut away the remainder. Once the icing has been completely trimmed, smooth the cut edges and remove the paper patterns.

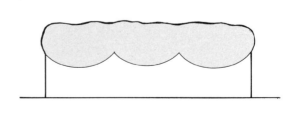

Allow the icing to dry out thoroughly. Decorate in the desired manner but do take advantage of ornaments which lend themselves to this style such as small picot edges or tassels piped on the cut edge.

Covering Hints

❑ Always ensure your icing is fresh.

❑ Do not knead your icing unless the work area has been cleaned otherwise small particles of cake may adhere to the icing.

❑ Do not roll out your icing until you have all your equipment at hand and your jam or glaze is heating gently. If there are long delays between rolling and application hairline cracks may result.

❑ Do not use too much icing sugar or cornflour when kneading and rolling out or cracks may fill with cornflour or icing sugar.

❑ Roll out the icing rather than just pressing and squashing it down. This will ensure a nice even thickness instead of lines and ridges.

❑ If the icing is not rolled out properly it will stick to the surface. Use rhythmic movements to achieve a good surface. Stand with legs slightly apart while rolling so that your weight will be distributed evenly. This will help you to roll your icing more evenly.

❑ When rolling icing keep lifting it to ensure it does not stick to the surface. You can dust the table with a little more icing or cornflour if required.

❑ Do not use icing which has tears at the corners or which is thin at one end and thick at the other. If this is the case, it is best to knead the icing once again and re-commence.

❑ If your covering is not quite right, it is always possible to remove it, re-knead and then begin again.

❑ Use a few drops of glycerine in your icing to help achieve a smooth finish.

❑ Do not cover cakes in the heat of the day.

❑ If your icing has been overworked, wrap it in plastic and place it in the freezer for a little while to revive it.

❑ If icing is too firm, it may still be used if kneaded with a batch of very soft icing.

❑ Remove small hairs or particles from iced cakes by using the tip of a pin.

❑ Do not store covered cakes in plastic containers or in rooms which are too damp or hot because the icing will sweat.

❑ Covered cakes will become damp and soggy if they are stored in the refrigerator.

❑ Do not make coverings too thin or staining may occur. The covering is also meant to ensure a smooth, even finish to the cake.

❑ Place a piece of greaseproof paper between the cake and the board.

❑ Ensure the cake and the paper adhere to the board by scraping a little royal icing on the board before setting the cake in place.

Once the icing has been placed on the cake do not work too hastily. This may cause accidents or damage to the cake. If accidental colour stains do occur while decorating, these should be treated immediately while still damp. They should be rubbed with pieces of white bread (do not use the crusts), which will absorb the unwanted colour. To carry out this procedure successfully, the cake icing must be dry. Other accidental marks can be treated in the same way.

SUMMER

Summer is a most popular season with its warmth and time for leisure and this is reflected in its celebrations. The flowers and golden grasses used in this section show the promise of summer with its long sunny days and relaxed living.

Flowers and decorations in this section reflect the flora that abounds in summer. Remember that the flowering season of many plants depends on the species, the climate and the location.

The flora of summer has been combined with appropriate cake shapes to enhance the seasonal theme. Cocoa butter painting and floodwork, used in unusual ways, have also been employed.

A ring cake combined with bright petunias and bougainvilleas provides a multi-purpose cake suitable for birthdays, weddings or even Christmas. Summer holidays at the beach can be celebrated with a beach ball cake using floodwork, while a stay in the mountains can be marked by a driftwood cake adorned with morning glories, plumbago and lobelia. For people holidaying in the country, surrounded by the golds and browns of drying grasses, a cake painted in cocoa butter is just the right choice. A heart with waterlilies makes a delightful engagement cake or a Valentine gift. Finally, a fan-shaped cake with a spray of fan-flowers, sun orchids and blue pincushions is a wonderfully nostalgic gift for an elderly aunt or grandmother.

Cocoa Butter Painting

This form of decorating enables you to reproduce pictures in sepia tones. Any picture requiring a monotone effect such as cameos, old bark huts, cottages and terrace houses is suitable for this medium. Old family photographs are · another source of inspiration especially if you are interested in genealogy. Imagine the decorative possibil-ities for a cake to celebrate that special centenary family reunion.

The methods used for this technique are very similar to floodwork. However, the materials used are cocoa butter, cocoa, and chocolate. It is necessary to keep the cocoa butter at a liquid consistency. The cocoa butter can be kept warm using a bain-marie method. Place the butter in a shallow bowl first, and then stand that in another bowl of hot water. This can then be placed under the strong light of a desk lamp to stop the water and butter from going cold too quickly. Change the water regularly so that it does not become too cold.

Depending on the picture you want it may be necessary to use a variety of cocoas to get different contrasts in tones. Cocoa is available in a wide range of colours, available from most chocolate or confectionery stores.

Mixing Colours

Place half a teaspoon of cocoa butter on the side of a shallow bowl. Melt it in the way described above. Use this bowl as an artist's palette, placing the different cocoas from left to right. Place a couple of dark compound chocolate buttons a little to the right of the butter, then add small quantities of different cocoas around the side. Be sure to keep some free space to allow for mixing.

To mix colours, dip a brush into the melted cocoa butter, and then into the melted chocolate. Work this on the free space until it is the required colour. Add more butter to lighten or more chocolate to darken the tone. The cocoa is mixed in the same way but it requires more mixing so that the particles dissolve in the cocoa butter. Wipe the brush on a warm, moist cloth between colour mixing so that the work remains clean and fresh.

Brushes

As the effects in this work are achieved by a variety of tones, it is also helpful to use a variety of brushes. Although this is not essential, it will make painting quicker and therefore reduce the number of times the water has to be changed.

A small, short, sable-hair, flat brush will be very effective for foliage, clouds and paths or roads. To achieve a very pale, almost ivory colour, take just a little chocolate on the very ends of the bristles and then load the brush with cocoa butter. Work this on the palette first to achieve an even tone, then brush onto the surface using either long, wide strokes for clouds, or short, rectangular strokes for foliage on trees. Be sure to leave some of the outer edges soft and blurred by using only a small amount of chocolate or butter.

This brush is also very useful for fence posts and railings as these can often be painted in just one stroke. Short, jump-like brush strokes, called stippling in china painting, can also be useful for graded shading. Make a small plaque to test these techniques before commencing on a cake.

A harder bristle brush can be used to achieve a layer effect similar to that of oil painting. These brushes are either round or flat, so experiment although only use the small sizes. Areas which may require a build up of cocoa or chocolate are items in the foreground, eyes, or hats and ribbons. The chocolate is more suitable for this work since it can be applied in a thicker coating than the cocoa.

Soft, regular sable-hair brushes are best for soft flowing areas such as drapery and hair. Flowers and dots are also best done with these brushes. Use all brushes in sizes ranging from numbers 0–6 but be aware that the same size number can vary considerably from brand to brand.

Painting with Cocoa

The application of cocoa onto the sugar surface can sometimes be difficult because of the particles. It is quite gritty and therefore does not flow as easily as the chocolate. Ensure the cocoa butter is as warm as possible. Work the cocoa onto the brush with some butter and then brush backwards and forwards on the bowl until it feels free and smooth. It will be necessary to repeat this process often but the result is very rewarding. Remember when painting with cocoa you need to use more cocoa butter than you do when working with chocolate.

Cocoa Butter Effects

Large areas such as sky, or the background to a cameo, can be painted with a very fine layer of cocoa butter to give an ivory finish to the work. A very faint tinge of brown can then be added to areas such as the horizon on a scene. In portraits, paint ivory tones to represent the source of light on the face or on the background. Brushes being used for cocoa butter painting often retain some chocolate or cocoa on the bristles even after they have been wiped. This can be used to advantage to give very soft brown shades but be sure to clean them thoroughly before using for the palest areas.

Once a cake has been decorated with a cocoa butter painting, allow it to dry thoroughly in a cool room or cupboard. Do not transport such a cake in the boot of a hot car because, in extreme cases, the chocolate may melt a little.

Sugar in Flight

It is traditional to pipe very small birds on wedding and engagement cakes. Included in the decorations, some birthday cakes often have a butterfly which has been piped, flooded or piped onto tulle.

The following adaptations are offered as an alternative to the above. Fine gossamer wings tipped in glitter add something magical to special occasions. These fragile adornments enhance transparent sugar flowers.

All of the following items can be piped either directly onto a cake or onto waxed paper, and then placed on a cake when the final finishing touches are being added.

Butterflies

(see colour plate opposite p. 33)

Before commencing this work, look at a book about butterflies. You will discover just how many varieties of butterfly there are and how the size and shape of the wings varies so much. Experiment a little to help in your selection of appropriate wing sizes and shapes.

Method

1 Take a small piece of rice paper and cut as many pairs of wings as required. Remember that the size of the wings will determine the size of the finished item. It is also possible to have just one wing on either side of the body instead of two.

2 Using some soft-peak royal icing (see p. 99), pipe a short body line onto the cake or paper. Be sure to allow a little more thickness for the head and the middle part of the body. Pipe two very short feelers on the head. To do this, place the tip of the tube to one side of the head, press the bag and without releasing the pressure pull away from the head. A short peak dot will remain. Repeat this on the other side of the head. Using a pair of tweezers place the wings on either side of the body giving them an appropriate slant. Set aside to dry thoroughly before continuing.

3 Brush each wing with a little water. This will allow the rice paper to bend and curve a little giving the wings a more realistic appearance rather than the straight inflexible lines they have when left dry. If the wings are to be coloured this can be done at the same time. Paint these in an appropriate colour or just lightly dust with a glittery powder.

Dragonflies

(see left colour plate between pp. 32–33)

These fragile-winged insects have been ignored by decorators in the past. However, the very delicate wings, and their varying size and colour, make them a pretty addition. In tropical zones, dragonflies are small and their bodies are red. Because waterlilies are common in the tropics dragonflies can be an appropriate addition to a cake adorned with these flowers.

Method

1 Take a small piece of rice paper and cut out two pairs of wings. Make the size of the wings appropriate to the size of the cake and the dragonfly. Obviously the larger the cake the larger the dragonfly can be.

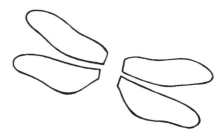

2 Using a soft-peak royal icing, pipe a body line on a piece of waxed paper or straight onto the cake. Insert the wings on either side of this line being sure to overlap part of the back wings with the front ones. Bend them at the required angle before the icing sets. Pipe another line over the main body line but leave the tail end narrow. Pipe two small feelers on the head as described in step 2 for Butterflies. Then set aside to dry thoroughly.

3 Using a fine sable-hair brush, moisten the wings all over with a little water. Paint the desired markings on all the wings. These can be just an outer edge of silver or gold. Alternatively, various vein marks can be lightly painted in the same colour. Perhaps experiment a little on a spare piece of rice paper. The water will soften the wings and help give them a more natural appearance.

Frills

Frills are also known as garrett frills or flounces. These frills are achieved by stretching a long or circular strip of soft icing so that it will frill or curl. The pieces are then attached to a covered cake in a variety of ways to achieve different effects.

The addition of these frills can be very useful. Once mastered, this work is easy and quick so it can be used on occasions when a cake is required in a hurry. Small cakes seem larger with the addition of frills. They can eliminate the need to pipe extension work, and they travel with fewer breakages. Since many brides choose wedding gowns with frills and flounces, this is yet another way of personalising a cake (see left colour plate between pp. 64–65).

If frills are to be used at the base of a cake, the cake itself will not require any embroidery at the bottom. It is, however, more attractive if there is a small snail trail peeping underneath. Other edges such as ribbon can also be attached if desired. All of this work must be done prior to attaching the frills.

Simple Frills

Method

1 Mark out a suitable pattern or line on the cake to which the frill can be attached. A line can be marked by running a pin along a ruler. It may be easiest to mark this line by using a piece of paper cut out to the same height and circumference as the cake. Fold the paper to mark where the frill is to be placed and then place it on the cake, marking the line with a pin.

2 If the frills are to be coloured, take a piece of soft icing and colour it. This can be done by adding a drop of liquid food colour or some grains of dry powder. Paste colours are also suitable for this work. Knead the paste until the colour has been thoroughly worked in, then form it into a ball and cut it in half. If the cut surface is evenly coloured then the paste is ready. Roll the paste out into a sausage shape and then roll this out as thinly as possible. Cut a scalloped strip to the required width allowing enough space for the embroidery design above the area to be frilled. It may be better to do the embroidery prior to the frilling.

join at the base will need to be hidden by adjusting the curves of the frill. Do not attempt this merging if the icing is hard and brittle.

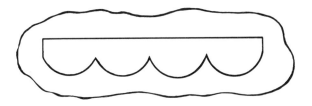

Scalloped Frills

3 Place the strip of soft icing on a board which has been lightly dusted with cornflour. Use a cocktail stick to frill the icing. The stick is held and pressed about 1 cm from the base edge of the icing. Roll back and forth taking care not to press too hard or the icing will tear. It will take a little practice to do this work but eventually you will develop a smooth technique. If the icing sticks, use a dry medium brush to gently ease it from the board. Repeat the process until all the base edge has been frilled. It will be necessary to move the paste along as it is worked so that it all becomes evenly curled. The icing will curl almost right up to the top of the strip but be careful to hold the stick so that the frilled edge remains the same depth all along. The icing curls because the base is enlarged while the top remains the same size. If long strips are to be treated, it is best to cover all areas not being worked to avoid drying and breakages.

Frills can be made with a scalloped base or top edge. There are various tools available for this work or you can use a number of scalloped biscuit cutters. These scalloped-edged frills are usually used when they are to be placed in a scallop pattern on the cake.

Method

1 Roll out a piece of soft icing as thinly as possible. Use the larger cutter to cut out the large scalloped circle and then cut out the centre by using the smaller one. The depth of the frill will depend on the difference in size of the cutters: if the inner cutter is small the frill will be deep, while a shallow frill is made by using a large inner cutter. To curl this doughnut shape, use a cocktail stick and the same method described in Simple Frills, step 3.

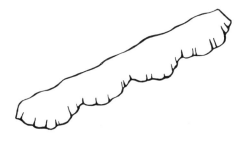

4 Brush a little water onto the cake just below the marked line and lift the frill onto a long, narrow piece of cardboard to aid in placing and to avoid tears. Press the top edge against the cake to secure it firmly. It is advisable to work as quickly as possible while frilling the icing. If it dries out too much it will crack and break. Although it is recommended that you turn the ends under on the frill before attaching it to the cake, it is also possible to work the joins together so that they merge at the top. The

2 These circles can be cut according to the size of the scallops required. A scalloped doughnut shape can be cut in two halves so that each is the same size as the scallops which have been previously marked on a cake. To achieve this it will be necessary to use an inner cutter which has a circumference twice as large as each scallop. Alternatively the doughnut can just have one cut so that it will fit around one scallop marked on the cake.

Frills made with these cutters tend to be fuller since the technique is similar to cutting fabric on the bias.

Embroidered Frills

Frills can be embroidered to make them look more like an addition of broderie-style lace. Since the very edge of these frills is usually a little frayed, it is best to add the embroidery to other areas of the frill.

Method

1 Once the strip of icing has been frilled it is possible to make a pattern of small holes at regular intervals to represent broderie anglaise. Use a fine bamboo skewer or the smallest hole in a leather punch to do this work. Remember to dip the tool into a little cornflour occasionally so that it does not tear at the icing. After a little practice it will be easier to use the punch for this work because it gives a regular-sized hole and is also much faster. Use some blue tack or something similar to attach a tape measure to the cake board. The tape can be used as a guide for spacing the pattern. Do not cut these holes too close to the edge, otherwise they may tear.

2 Attach the frills to the cake in the same way as described in Simple Frills, step 4.

3 Once the frills have dried, use a fine icing tube to embroider the outer edge of these small holes with royal icing. Pipe any other decorations and then set the cake aside to allow them to dry.

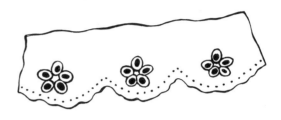

Tinted Embroidered Frills

Method

1 Follow the instructions for Embroidered Frills to the end of step 3.

2 After the cake has dried, use a dry brush to tint either all the frill or just the base edge. If frosted petal dust is available this will be more effective. Brush a small amount of dry powder along the base edge of the frills but be careful not to tear them. After this has been completed, clean the brush and then brush away any excess dust which is on the base of the board.

3 If a deeper edge is required, it is possible to use liquid colours for this tinting. When liquid colour is to be used, allow the brush to just touch the tip of the frill so that it absorbs the colour and therefore spreads a little. Any excess liquid on the brush can be soaked up onto a dry cloth before applying it to the cake.

Very small, shallow frills can be made for other special purposes. An example of this would be layers of frills on the petticoat of a flooded figure, frills on a bonnet, or the lace around a posy of flowers.

Frills can be attached in layers to give an even fuller appearance. Arrange these by placing the base one first and then working up.

Shells

Sugar shells are as easy to make as sugar flowers. It is advisable to collect samples of a variety of shells so that realistic results can be achieved.

Instructions are given for a small selection of shells, including bivalves and univalves. Note shells are much thicker than flower petals. Be careful not to make them too thick, however, or they will not be as pretty. After a shell has been completed it is advisable to drop it into a jar or bowl of cornflour so that it dries in the correct shape. Shells or sugar ornaments which are left to dry on a board or similar tend to go flat on the underside. When colouring the shells, remember to keep a realistic colour scheme that blends well. If your shells need to be glossy, they can be painted with an Edible Gloss (see p. 99) after they are completely dry.

Scallop Shells

(see colour plate opposite p. 17)

These shells can be found in many parts of the world. Often, they are treated and sold in kitchen stores for presentation of seafoods. Depending on the region where the shells are found, they may consist of one deeply curved shell matched with a flat one or they may be an identical pair of slightly flatter shells.

Method

1 Take a piece of paste large enough to make one shell and roll it out to about 1–2 mm in thickness. Lightly dust the inside of the shell with cornflour and then press the paste onto this. Press firmly enough to indent the paste but be careful it does not break. Cut away the excess paste by rubbing against the edges using a downward motion.

2 Neaten the edges by pressing against the sides making sure the paste remains smooth and even. Allow the paste to remain in the shell for 30–60 minutes so it takes on the curved shape. Remove the sugar shell and set aside for a further 12 hours to dry thoroughly before colouring.

These shells can be painted in shades of grey, mauve, musk, pink or pale gold.

Ark Shells

(see colour plate opposite p. 17)

Many of the shells in this family are quite elongated, with a series of teeth at the hinge. They have a pattern of lines in both directions. Along the length these lines sometimes form colour bands, while those which commence near the hinge radiate down in a pattern of wedge-like divisions. Some of these shells have folds which give the impression of a four-sided shell.

Method

1 Take a piece of paste which is large enough to make one shell when rolled out to a thickness of 1–2 mm. Lightly dust the outside of a shell with cornflour and then lay the paste over the top. Tear away the excess paste using a downward movement, and then smooth the edges by rubbing with the fingers.

2 Repeat the directions given in step 1 to make the second half of this bivalve. Allow both to dry for 30–60 minutes and then remove and allow another 12 hours for complete drying. If the linear patterns are to be indented into the paste, this should be done while it is still moist. Alternatively, these patterns can be painted onto the surface after it is completely dry. Colour the shells in ivory or pale gold and then paint a series of wavy patterns to represent the natural colour bands found on these shells. The bands are usually in tones of deep gold or graded shades of brown.

Note that the two halves to this shell are not identical.

29

Auger Shells

(see colour plate opposite p. 17)

Method

1 Take a piece of paste which is long enough to form a very thin, narrow cone. If a sample shell is not available, make a cone which is 12 mm at the widest part and 6 cm in length. To produce a cone, roll the paste between the palms being sure to place pressure only at one end. Pinch at the pointed tip and use a clockwise motion to twist the other end.

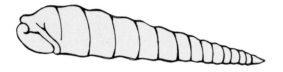

2 Insert a suitable tool into the twisted end to form a small cavity. Some varieties of augers have a series of lines spiralling along the length but these can be achieved with colouring if preferred. Allow the shell to dry and then colour in shades of brown, gold or ivory.

Olive Shells

(see colour plate opposite p. 17)

Method

Take a piece of paste large enough to form a small oval or olive shape. A recommended size is 1.5 cm in width by 3.5 cm in length. Pinch along one side for two-thirds the length of the paste forming a flat outer flap. Curve this around the solid olive to represent the shell opening. Ensure the top has a small, shallow point and use a tool at the base to indent a small hole. Mark two curved lines along the curve of the base and then drop the olive into cornflour. Allow to dry thoroughly before colouring in tones of brown, gold, mauve or ivory.

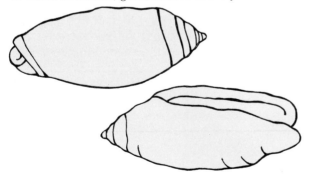

Conch shells

(see colour plate opposite p. 17)

Method

1 Take a piece of paste which is large enough to form a cone about 4 cm in length and 2 cm in width. Pull and pinch at one end to form a short point which is just a little less than half the length of the cone. Form the lip on the right edge of the cone commencing about halfway down the length. Pinch at the edge to form a flat section about 1 cm in width and then curve it a little way round the solid part of the shell. The lip slants back just at the base, and spiralling lines can be marked around the pointed top of the cone.

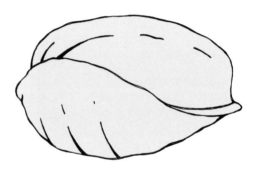

2 Colour the shell once it is completely dry. Most conch shells have gold markings in patterns which rotate around the shell.

Flower Moulding

The flowers offered in this book can be made from any of the paste or gum recipes on pp. 97–98. The term 'moulded' refers to the fact that this sugar paste is pulled, shaped and cut into the various forms required.

Most of the recipes require the paste to be 'worked up'. This means kneading it to a workable consistency. Some recipes require the paste to be kneaded with a quantity of cornflour so that it becomes pliable and firm. A paste is at the right consistency if it is firm and not sticky, but soft enough to have some 'give' so that it does not crack and break when it is curved and bent. *Since all of these pastes dry out very quickly, it is important to use only a little at a time. Place the remainder in a plastic bag until it is ready to be used.*

Depending on the flower, one or several of the following techniques are used during the making process.

Cutting

Individual petals are made separately by rolling out a piece of paste until it is very thin. Cut petals out of this by using either a cutter or a template.

Shaping

Petals can be made by taking a small quantity of paste which is then flattened between the fingers until the desired shape and size have been produced. These petals can be trimmed with a small pair of scissors to remove any frayed edges and to achieve a uniform size and shape.

Hollowing

This method is used for flowers of varying sizes. Whether they are very small and fine or large and thicker, the method will still be the same. Take a piece of paste between the fingers and, using a rolling technique, shape it into a teardrop. It is then necessary to use a cocktail stick, the handle of a brush or any other suitable tool. Insert this tool into the centre of the teardrop cone, using a backwards and forwards motion. Allow the paste to be hollowed out while leaving the edges thin and even. Once the cone is large enough, use your fingers to smooth out the shape when making a larger flower.

Fluting or Frilling

This is the term used for the soft, curved look which many petals require. Many varieties of flowers have soft, frilly petals which are a distinctive feature. Once the petal has been cut from the paste it is then fluted or frilled. Drape it over a finger (or place it on a work surface) then, with the aid of a cocktail stick or the handle of a paint brush, press the edges to thin them down. It will be necessary to roll the handle backwards and forwards while continually moving the petal. Continue until all the edges have been worked in this way. The frill or fluted effect is achieved by the outer surface being enlarged while the centre remains the same as it was at the start.

Balling

This method gets its name from the tool used for the technique. However, many pottery tools are also very suitable for this work. To ball a petal, place it in the palm of the hand and then use a rolling and pushing motion to work around the edge. This method curves and thins the edges of petals and flowers and is similar to frilling but gives a less frilly effect. It is important to do this work while the petal is still moist, otherwise it will crack.

Cupping

This can be done by placing the petal in the palm of the hand and then pressing with the thumb. Alternatively the petal can be placed on a piece of foam and then the centre pressed with the thumb to give a curved shape.

Moulded Flowers

Blue Pincushion*

(see colour plate opposite p. 33)

Often seen as a mass of blue across a field, these Australian natives are beautiful flowers. Each bloom is a mass of florets within one flower. Depending on soil and location, they can vary in colour from the palest sky blue to a very deep corn-flower blue.

Flower

Method

1   This flower is made from a combination of moulded and piped sugar work. To commence, take a ball of paste about 12 mm in diameter. Mould this between the fingers to form a shallow cone with only a slightly rounded top. This cone should be 12 mm × 12 mm. It will not be necessary to hollow it out.

2   Take a 12–15 cm piece of fine or medium cotton-covered wire and make a small hook at one end. Moisten this and insert it into the base of the cone and pinch so that it is firmly secured.

3   Fill an icing bag with a firm royal icing and cut a small hole at the tip. Pipe a series of drag leaves all over the top of the cone and down the sides a little. This top head of spiked-looking leaves should be about 7 mm in height if it is measured from the side to the top. To give the leaves a spiked look, commence by placing the tip of the icing bag against the crown of the cone. Squeeze and press the icing so that it forms a medium-sized dot on the crown. Still pushing, allow the icing to continue to flow for a little. Stop pressing, and then pull up and away from the cone all in the one sharp movement. This will need to be repeated until the desired shape has been formed.

*Brunonia astralis

4   Before the icing dries, use a pair of tweezers to insert many short fine stamens into this mass of spiked leaves. They should be long enough to stand a little taller than the leaves. Repeat the process for all the flowers required and then set them aside to dry thoroughly before continuing.

Calyx

Method

Roll out a piece of paste as thinly as possible. Using the pattern below, cut out several sepals. Brush a little water along the inside of the sepals leaving the top 5 mm dry. Attach the wet base of the sepal to the base of the flower and then pull the tip of the sepal back away from the flower. Press gently along the length of the sepals to ensure that they attach firmly.

No leaves or buds are required for this flower.

Bougainvillea

(see colour plate opposite)

Although these plants belong to tropical and sub-tropical environments, many are grown successfully in other locations. There is a misconception

This ring-shaped cake is decorated with magenta bougainvillea and white petunias. The contrast in colours helps to create the crisp, light touch of summer. The embroidery work represents bougainvillea in cross stitch. When covering the cake, roll out the icing and remove a small circular piece from the middle – after placing the icing on the cake it will be easier to work the icing down the central hole. (Instructions: Cake Shapes, p.15; Bougainvillea, p.32; Petunia, p.36; Cross Stitch, p.48; Presenting Flowers, p.82; Cake Designs, p.100.)

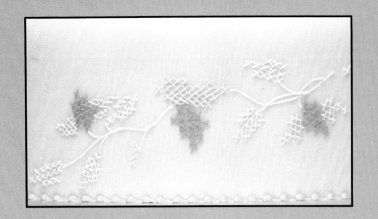

ABOVE: A cake in the form of a piece of driftwood allows a more natural presentation of flowers. Those selected are morning glories, pale blue plumbago and lobelia in blue and white – all grow in great profusion and their tendency to climb and scramble over everything makes them ideal for this cake. (Instructions: Cake Shapes, p.15; Lobelia, p.34; Morning Glory, p.35; Plumbago, p.37; Presenting Flowers, p.82.)

OPPOSITE: Heart-shaped cakes are ideal for romantic celebrations. The surface of the cake is used to advantage to suggest a lake on which waterlilies, flushed with pink, appear to float. The lace pieces for the side have been made in the shape of small waterlilies. These flowers and red dragonflies, associated with the tropics, combine to reinforce the summer theme. (Instructions: Cake Shapes, p.15; Dragonflies, p.25; Waterlily, p.39; Lace, p.52; Gift Cards, p.68.)

regarding the flower of this plant: the showy triple-petal 'flower' is actually the floral bract. The real flowers are insignificant, small, cream, star-like centres of the floral bract. Instructions include both the floral bracts and the flower, the whole of which will be referred to as the flower. Presented in trailing masses, these flowers are yet another beautiful addition to cake decorating.

Flower

The cream flowers can be presented as tight knobs on the ends of long stamens.

Method

Take three stamens which are 2–3 cm in length. Take a small quantity of paste and insert a small knob on each of the three stamen ends. Use a pair of tweezers to pinch and mark the paste so that it looks like a small, four-petal star. Curve each of the stamens and then attach the lower ends onto a piece of paste. Twist and squeeze the paste until it is attached firmly. Insert the moistened and hooked end of a piece of medium cotton-covered wire. Squeeze and press so that the stem becomes firmly attached.

Floral Bracts

Method

1 Take a piece of paste and roll it out as thinly as possible. Using the pattern below, cut out three

petals from the paste. Indent a veined pattern into each of these and then gently ball the outer edges.

2 Take one of the stamen centres which have been made. Moisten the base of the three petals and then assemble them into a triangular flower placing the stamen section in the middle. Press and squeeze these together so that the base is neat and firm. Bend and curve the petals in an outward slant.

Leaf

Method

Roll out a piece of paste so that it is very thin at one end and slightly thicker at the other. Cut out a leaf using the pattern below. Vein the leaf and then insert a hooked piece of fine cotton-covered wire into the thick top end to form the stem. Bend and curve the leaf and set it aside to dry. Make several of these so that a realistic representation can be achieved.

Although fans belong to a past era, their shape makes them suitable for many celebratory cakes. The spray of summer flowers includes dune fan-flowers, blue pincushions and sun orchids. Rows of scalloped and embroidered sugar frills create a pretty, feminine effect and also accentuate the downwards slant of the top of the cake. The embroidery work around the sides is a simple design of flowers and scallops. Translucent butterflies add a final touch. (Instructions: Cake Shapes, p. 15; Butterflies, p. 25; Frills, p. 26; Blue Pincushion, p. 32; Fan-flower, p. 34; Sun Orchid, p. 38; Embroidery, p. 43; Scallops, p. 45; Presenting Flowers, p. 82.)

Fan-flower*

(see colour plate opposite p. 33)

These flowers are usually found in Australian coastal regions. Depending on the variety, flowers can be either small or large although they all have the same fan-like appearance. They come in shades of blue, pink and mauve.

Flower

Method

1 Take a ball of paste about 8 mm in diameter and roll it between the fingers shaping it into a small teardrop about 1 cm in length. Take a 12–15 cm piece of fine or medium cotton-covered wire and make a small hook at one end. Moisten this end and insert it into the base of the teardrop being sure to pinch the base to secure it firmly.

2 Hollow out the paste either with the handle of a brush or with another suitable tool. The cone should be fine, with a depth of about 1.5 cm.

3 Cut away a wedge of the cone so that the base remains intact. Retain between half and two-thirds of the cone. Divide the remaining area into five, equal-sized petals. These incisions should be at least 1 cm in length.

4 Trim each petal so that it is softly curved on the sides and the tip is a soft, rounded point. Indent a very soft, central vein along the length of the petals.

5 Insert the brush handle into the centre of the flower base and push in a little. This will give the flower a little more depth. Set aside to dry thoroughly before colouring.

No buds or leaves are required for this flower.

*Scaevola species

Lobelia

(see right colour plate between pp. 32–33)

This is a most attractive flower. It is usually seen as a border plant and, although it appears in a range of colours, it is usually known as blue lobelia. This is not a commonly used flower in cake decorating. However, it offers many possibilities because of its beautiful blue tones and trailing habit.

Flower

This flower is made from a hollowed cone shape although much of the paste is cut away so that the flower appears to have only three petals.

Method

1 Take a ball of paste which is about 7 mm in diameter. Roll this between the fingers to form a teardrop shape which is about 1 cm in length. Using a suitable tool or the handle of a paint brush hollow out the centre.

2 Take a 12–15 cm piece of fine cotton-covered wire and form a hook at one end. Moisten this end before attaching it to the cone. Shake off any excess water and then pinch the paste at the base so that it is attached securely and neatly.

3 Cut away two-thirds of the outer part of the cone. Be sure to leave some length in the base otherwise there will be nothing with which to support the completed flower.

4 Cut the remainder of the cone into three equal petals. These are quite deep, measuring 5–7 mm. Trim a little off the outer edges of the petals to give them a soft, rounded point. Lay the flower on a piece of rubber and then roll a cocktail stick along the outer edges of the petals. Use the back of a blade of a pair of scissors to give a soft line indentation along the length of each petal.

5 Insert the tip of a cocktail stick into the centre of the base of the cone. Push the paste a little forward at this point making sure that it is directly opposite the three petals. Squeeze and pinch this paste until it is 4 mm in length. Cut this into a pair of very small petals which stand upright, cutting away any excess paste. Make several flowers and then set them aside to dry.

Calyx

Method

Take a freshly made flower which is still moist. Use a pair of fine, small scissors to make five incisions into the cone-shaped base of the flower. Take care the incisions are evenly spaced. Five sepals, representing the calyx, will be formed. It is necessary to cut enough of the paste to form very fine, long, pointed sepals which are still attached to the flower. Do not cut the paste off the flower.

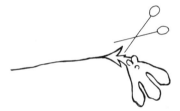

Buds

Method

Take a 15 cm piece of fine or medium cotton-covered wire and insert it into a small ball of paste about 4 mm in diameter. Press and squeeze to attach firmly, then press and flatten the top to form a blunt-looking, cone-like bud. Make the calyx in the same way described above.

Morning Glory

(see right colour plate between pp. 32–33)

These trailing and climbing plants have attractive masses of white or blue-purple trumpet-shaped flowers.

Flower

Since life-sized replicas of this flower are too large, the instructions provided will produce decorations which are about two-thirds the size of the real flower.

Method

1 Take a ball of paste which is 1.5–2 cm in diameter and roll this between the fingers to form a cone. Hollow and thin this with the aid of a thick paint brush handle. As with other larger flowers, it is possible to thin and enlarge this cone by pressing the top edges between the fingers during the latter part of the process.

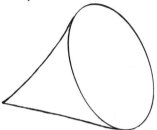

2 Once the cone has been hollowed, insert the paint brush handle into the centre and apply pressure to the base of the flower. This will produce a true trumpet shape at the base of the hollowed cone. Use a thinner paint brush handle or a cocktail stick to lightly frill or flute the top edges of the flower. Do not frill this flower too much.

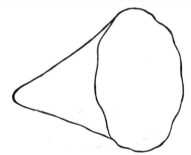

3 Use the back of a knife blade or any other suitable tool to indent a star pattern on the inside of the flower. Be sure to mark the points of the star to the top edge of the paste. Make several of these and set them aside to dry before colouring.

Leaf

Method

1 Take a piece of paste and roll it out thinly leaving one side slightly thicker than the other. This is necessary to ensure that there is thickness into which the wire can be placed. Cut out a number of leaves using the patterns below.

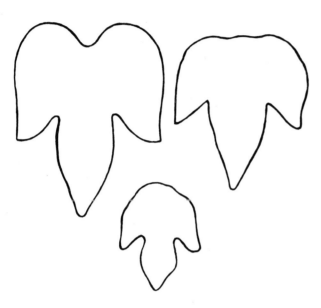

2 Insert a moistened hooked piece of wire into the top of the leaves. Pinch and squeeze the paste to attach securely. Vein the leaves and then set aside to dry. It is advisable to drape the leaf in, or over, suitably shaped pieces of foil.

Petunia

(see colour plate opposite p. 32)

Petunias are beautiful summer flowers which come in a large range of colours. Some can be quite large so, although they may look wonderful in the garden, it is wise to scale them down according to the size of the cake on which they are to be used.

Flower

Method

1 Before commencing, note that the completed flower will be 3–4 cm in both depth and width. If a larger or smaller flower is required, use paste quantity according to your needs.

Take a ball of paste which is about 1.5 cm in diameter and roll this between the fingers to form a teardrop which is 3 cm in length and 1 cm in width at one end. Take a 15–18 cm piece of medium cotton-covered wire and make a small hook at one end. Moisten the hooked end and insert it into the base of the teardrop being sure to pinch and squeeze at the base so that it is attached securely.

2 Hollow out the cone using the handle of a brush or some other suitable tool. Once the cone is large enough it will be possible to continue this hollowing and thinning by squeezing the paste between the fingers. As this part of the flower is being made, it may be necessary to revert to the use of the handle occasionally. If the cone appears to have a long and narrow base with only the top opening out, insert the handle down the centre and hollow out the cone with the handle again. Repeat this process until the hollowed cone is 3–4 cm in depth and width. It is important that the base is narrower than the top.

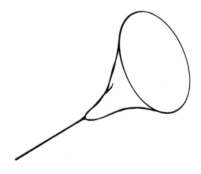

3 Now you need to frill the outer edges of the flower. Place the flower on a piece of rubber and roll a cocktail stick backwards and forwards along the edges of the cone repeating the process long enough to give the flower a very curly, frilled edge. Adjust the pressure while doing this, otherwise the flower will tear. Once the cone has been completely frilled, the flower is ready to set aside for drying.

No buds or leaves are required for this flower.

Plumbago

(see right colour plate between pp. 32–33)

This is a beautiful, dense shrub with clusters of pale blue or white flowers. The flowers grow in round clusters and, even when fully in season, there are always many buds within these clusters. Buds and flowers have very long and slender bases.

Flower

Method

1 Take a ball of paste about 9 mm in diameter. Make a small hook at one end of a 12–15 cm length of fine or medium cotton-covered wire. Roll the paste between the fingers to form a long, slender-based cone.

2 Hollow out the top part of the cone but retain the length in the base. The diameter of the hollowed cone should be 2 cm and the length of the base part of the cone should be 1.5 cm. This hollowing can be done with a suitable tool or with the handle of a paint brush.

3 Insert the hooked end of the wire, which has already been moistened, into the centre of the cone. Pull the wire through the length of the narrow base of the cone. Pinch and squeeze the paste at the base to ensure it is attached firmly. If the paste looks too fat for a realistic replica of the flower, roll the base between the fingers. This will

elongate and thin the paste along the wire at the base of the flower. Cut off any unwanted length.

4 Cut and divide the top part of the cone into five equal petals. These incisions will be very deep, about 8 mm, so that the petals appear to have the wide spacing that nature gives them. Trim these petals by cutting the excess paste away from each side. The final appearance is a rounded petal with a very shallow, slightly pointed tip. These flowers have a very pronounced, deeper colour line down the centre. The best way to duplicate this is to make a light indentation down the centre length of each petal. Do this with the blunt side of a knife blade.

5 Using the blade of a pair of scissors, push it down between each petal, pressing a little into the centre base of the flower. This will help increase the depth of the divisions, thus making each petal appear to be attached only at the base. Make several of these flowers in graded sizes to give the final cluster a realistic appearance.

Buds

Method

1 These buds are very slender and long so the bulk of the paste will be placed along the wire. Take a ball of paste which is 4 mm in diameter. Take a 12–15 cm length of fine cotton-covered wire and make a small hook at one end. Moisten this end, removing any excess water, and then insert it into the paste.

2 Roll the paste between the fingers so that it thins and adheres to the wire. The tip of the bud is only slightly fatter than the remainder. Buds can vary in length from 1–3 cm but, regardless of length, they should all look very slender.

Leaf

Method

Take some paste and roll it out. It should be thin at one end and thicker at the other. Cut out several leaves using the patterns below. Attach wires as stems, bend and curve them and then set aside to dry before colouring. Sometimes a more realistic effect can be achieved by lightly balling the outer leaf edges.

*Sun Orchid**

(see colour plate opposite p. 33)

These orchids are small, Australian native flowers. Depending on the variety, they can be blue, gold or salmon in colour.

Flower

Method

1 Take a ball of paste which is 1 cm in diameter and roll it between the fingers to form a teardrop. Hollow out the paste using the handle of a paint brush, thinning the cone as evenly as possible. The hollowed cone should be about 1.5 cm in depth as well as width.

2 The cone needs to be divided into six sections. Make one larger than the rest to use as the trumpet of the flower. Cut the largest petal and then divide the remainder into five equal petals.

3 Trim each petal so that it is softly rounded with a very slight point at the tip. The base trumpet will be more rounded. Press and squeeze the petals between the fingers so that they become thinner, then pinch the tip. The top petal will need to curve forward towards the trumpet while the others need have only the slightest inward curve. The base trumpet or petal should be only a little larger than the others. It can be curved slightly by running a paint brush handle from left to right along the outer part of the petal.

4 Take a 15 cm piece of fine or medium cotton-covered wire and make a small hook at one end. Moisten the hooked end and insert it into the flower from the centre through to the back. Pinch the paste at the base to secure it neatly.

5 Take another piece of paste, about 3 cm in thickness. This piece will form the tongue of the flower. Roll this into a small ball and then press the end of a paint brush handle against it. It will be necessary to allow the paste to wrap around the end of the handle so that the edge of the tongue has a curve.

6 Trim and straighten the base of this tongue by cutting it to form a straight line. Pinch the tip and moisten the base. Moisten the centre of the flower also but be sure not to use too much water. Using the brush, insert the tongue so that the curve slants in towards the trumpet. Be sure to press firmly so that the paste will attach itself securely.

*Thelymitra species

Waterlily

(see left colour plate between pp. 32–33)

These plants can be divided into two different groups: the hardy variety which grow in cooler climates; and the tropical plants, some of which produce small star-like flowers. You can produce very attractive and elegant presentations with this flower.

Flower

Method

1 A set of waterlily cutters will be invaluable when making this flower. These cutters are available in sets of three or four. All have the same shape but they are graded in size. Alternatively, cutters can be made using the patterns below.

2 Roll out some paste on a tile or some other suitable surface making it as thin and even as possible. It is best to roll out enough paste to cut out all the petals required for each layer. This method will give your petals uniform texture, thus enabling the finished flower to look very delicate. Using the smallest cutter, cut out 7–9 petals. Each of these petals will need to be curved in the following way. Place a petal in the palm of the hand and place the handle of a paint brush along the centre of its length. Roll the brush from left to right until the petal is curved. Place each petal on a suitably curved piece of foil and then slightly bend the centre of the foil. This bend should tilt the petal ends inward. The completed petals will have the appearance of concave banana shapes.

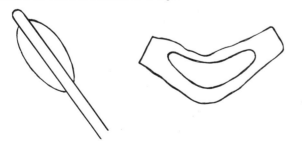

3 Using the next size petal cutter, cut out another set of petals. Cut 7–10 petals and curve them in the same way described in step 2 above. Set these aside on foil. These petals will have the same shape and curve as the previous ones.

4 Using the third cutter, roll out more paste and cut out another layer of 9 or 10 petals. Curve and bend in the same way as the others.

5 If an extra large flower is required, a fourth layer of petals can be made. If you only have three different-sized cutters, it will be best to make only three layers. If a fourth layer is to be made, cut òut 11–13 petals from another piece of paste and curve and bend them using the same method described above. Set all petals aside to dry thoroughly before assembling.

6 Take a piece of foil large enough to hold the completed flower. The smaller version measures 8 cm in diameter. Pipe a large ball of firm royal icing in the centre of the foil. Arrange the smallest petals in a circle, setting them into the icing. If you overlap these partially to allow for a fuller looking centre you will use a greater number of petals. The centre petals will need to slant upwards to give the flower its distinct illusion of height. Arrange the second layer of petals under the first. Many of these petals will be placed below and between those already in position. If more icing is required, this can be piped onto the foil in another outer circle or onto the base of each petal. Insert the third row in the same way as the second.

7 Cut several stamens to about 1 cm in length. Bend and curve these and then attach them to the centre using a pair of tweezers to ensure a compact, full cluster of stamens. You need to see as little icing as possible between these, so quite a large number of stamens is required.

Buds

Buds need to be made in a size which complements the flowers. For this reason it is best to make the buds after the flowers have been assembled.

Method

1   If no stems are required for the buds, the bases will need to be slightly flattened so that the buds can be placed upright on the cake. This presentation will make both the flower and buds appear more realistic. Buds requiring stems should be made with a short piece of heavy cotton-covered wire. This will need to be encased in a covering of paste to make the stem thicker.

Take a ball of paste which is 2–3 cm in diameter and roll it between the fingers to form a bud shape 2 cm in diamter and 3 cm in length. The tip of the bud should have a soft, rounded top. Slightly flatten the base by pressing down on a flat surface.

2   Take a piece of paste and roll it out as thinly as possible. Cut out four sepals using the pattern below. Moisten one side of each and then attach them to the bud placing the sepals in pairs opposite each other.

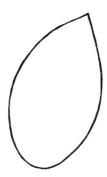

3   This step is only required if a stem is needed. Insert the hooked end of a piece of heavy cotton-covered wire into the base of the bud and pinch and squeeze it to attach the wire securely. Take a

piece of paste and roll it into a sausage which is as long as the wire. Press this against the wire until it covers and thickens the stem. It is desirable to bend the wire into the required shape now because once the paste has dried it will crack. This paste-covered wire can either be coloured or covered with florist's tape once it is dry.

Leaf

Leaves, more commonly known as lily pads, are very simple to make and give a touch of reality to an arrangement.

Method

1   The completed leaves will be 3–5 cm in diameter so they are in proportion to the flower which has been described. However, larger leaves can be presented with these flowers, if they are to be placed on a large cake.

Take a piece of paste and roll it out on the surface of a tile or other suitable material. Allow the centre of this paste to be just a little thicker than the outer part. Use a suitable cutter, a small biscuit cutter, or a small sherry glass to cut out a circle which is 3–5 cm in diameter. Cut out a small wedge from this circle but be sure not to cut right into the centre.

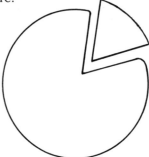

2   Using any suitable tool, indent veins into the surface of the leaf. The central vein is slightly heavier than all the others, giving the leaf the appearance of being divided in half. All other veins radiate from the centre of the leaf or from where the corner of the wedge was removed. Gently frill or ball the outer edges to gives the leaves a more realistic appearance.

Grasses

As summer progresses, the dry, hot days bring with them the grace and beauty of tall slender grasses which turn from the rich greens of spring to shades of gold and brown. Many of these grasses can combine beautifully with exotic and native flowers. Their colours also offer a pleasant addition to the more traditional flower arrangements. Grasses can be moulded or piped. Moulded grasses are first.

Oats

(see colour plate opposite p. 16)

There are many varieties of this annual grass. However, for the purposes of this book the spent seed stage of the grass is the one that is represented.

Spent Seeds

Method

1 Take a piece of fine or medium cotton-covered wire which is about 12–15 cm in length. Make a small hook at one end and moisten it before inserting into a very small ball of paste. Press and squeeze the paste to attach it firmly. This does not form part of the grass but is used as an anchoring piece.

2 Take some paste and roll it out as thinly as possible. Using the pattern below, cut out two petals. Ball the centre of these so that they stretch and curve along the length. Moisten the base tip of both petals and then attach them to the wire being sure to place them opposite each other. Pinch the bases of both petals to ensure they are secure, then pull the petals into a suitable shape. These seeds are usually open with the petal section curved and sometimes bent in the middle. Make several of these in various shapes so that when combined they appear natural.

Common Plantain

(see colour plate opposite p. 16)

These seedheads look like pretty flowers in tones of dark brown which look almost black. These tones contrast with the pale gold pollen grains found on the stamens which surround the base of the flower. Instructions are given only for the flowers.

Flower

Method

1 Take a of fine or medium cotton-covered wire, about 15 cm in length. Make a small hook at one end and moisten the hooked end in water. Take a ball of paste about 1 cm in diameter. Roll this between the fingers until a bullet shape about 2.5 cm long has been made. Roll this over a medium-surface grater to indent small ripples on the bullet-shaped paste. Insert the wire at the fatter end and press and squeeze the paste at the wire end so that it becomes attached securely.

2 Take as many as 30 fine-tipped stamens which are 5–8 mm in length. Pull each of these between the thumb and finger to curve them. Insert these around the lower portion of the flower to form a three or four level circle or skirt around the flower. Note that the top half of the flower has no stamens, and neither does the bottom of the base. Make these flowers in varied sizes ranging from 1.5–3 cm in length.

The following three grasses are piped onto wire using royal icing (see p. 99).

Perennial Ryegrass

(see colour plate opposite p. 16)

Method

1 Take a piece of medium cotton-covered wire about 20–25 cm in length. Bend and very gently curve it, then moisten the entire length with water. Lay the wire flat on a piece of waxed paper.

2 Use a piping bag filled with soft-peak royal icing to pipe a series of elongated drag leaves along both sides of the wire. The bag can be fitted with a 00 tube, or the tip of the bag can be cut off, leaving a small hole. These leaves should be piped at a 45-degree angle to the wire. Use a forwards and backwards movement to give each leaf some detail lines. Do not pipe leaves along the entire length of the wire because it will be impossible to place the stem in an arrangement without breaking the lower leaves.

Slender Cane Grass

(see colour plate opposite p. 16)

Method

1 Take a 20–25 cm piece of medium cotton-covered wire and bend it to a soft, gentle curve. Take two 10 cm pieces of nylon-covered wire and attach these to the main stem in the following way. Hold one length of the nylon-covered wire so that it forms a T-junction 5 cm from the top of the central stem. Twist the short wire around the central stem so that it becomes attached in the middle. Repeat this process with the second piece of nylon-covered wire, 5 cm below the first join. Bend all the fine wires so that they form curved pairs to the right of the central stem. Curve these a little and arrange them so that each pair is slanted downwards.

2 Fill an icing bag with soft-peak royal icing and then cut a very small hole at the tip. Pipe a series of slightly pointed dots along the entire length of the fine wires as well as along the top 5 cm of the thicker wire. Allow to dry and then turn the stem

over and repipe the dots on the back of the dry ones to give a three-dimensional effect. Set aside to dry thoroughly.

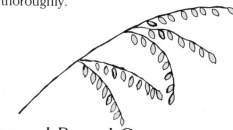

Annual Beard Grass

(see colour plate opposite p. 16)

There are many grasses which have these tufted looking flower heads. Some are soft and fluffy with very fine hairs, while others have distinctly spiked seedheads forming the cluster.

Method

1 Take a 20–25 cm piece of medium cotton-covered wire. Attach a piece of paste to one end and roll this between the fingers to form it into a bullet shape about 1 cm in width and 3.5 cm in length.

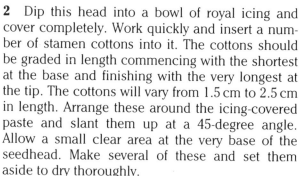

2 Dip this head into a bowl of royal icing and cover completely. Work quickly and insert a number of stamen cottons into it. The cottons should be graded in length commencing with the shortest at the base and finishing with the very longest at the tip. The cottons will vary from 1.5 cm to 2.5 cm in length. Arrange these around the icing-covered paste and slant them up at a 45-degree angle. Allow a small clear area at the very base of the seedhead. Make several of these and set them aside to dry thoroughly.

Hopefully the cakes presented in this section will encourage you to seek original and appropriate shapes for your summer cakes and to try freestyle designs that lend themselves to the particular flowers of the season. There are many flowers not presented in this section that can give you further ideas for cake designs.

AUTUMN

Autumn is a time for reflecting and harvesting, the season of fine mellow wines. It brings days of strong, bright colours: blue skies contrasted with the brilliant golds and russets of falling leaves.

Not surprisingly, autumn offers a wonderful collection of cakes and decorations suitable for special occasions such as retirements and anniversaries.

The flowers and decorations in this section reflect the usual flora of the season although there may be some variations depending on location. Flowering periods may also vary according to climate.

Although many of the cakes in this section have been designed to be multi-purpose they are especially suitable for celebrating the later milestones in the cycle of life such as retirement. Autumn leaves on a cake can be used for birthdays, anniversaries and retirements. Chrysanthemums on a ginger jar cake can be used for many occasions, including weddings and Mothers' Day. Candles are synonymous with birthdays so a candle-shaped cake is ideal for such celebrations. Cakes depicting autumn scenes are particularly versatile because in addition to their general uses they can celebrate the events, such as harvest time, which they reflect. The two-tier wedding cake cannot be mistaken for anything else, but how wonderful to have a cake fashioned in the style of a bride's gown and adorned with camellias and the bright gold of nerines.

Embroidery

This delicate work is wonderfully versatile. It can be done in white or coloured icing and it can be very simple or elaborate. It can reproduce a small pattern to complement moulded decorations. Occasionally a combination of small flooded or painted decorations is used within small areas of embroidery. Some designs include the addition of smaller moulded flowers with a spray of embroidered work. Ribbons and lace are often included to achieve a beautiful finished effect. Any form of embroidery may be used on any type of iced cake. Informal occasions such as afternoon tea can be enhanced by wonderfully decorated cakes. Embroidery may be used on the top or side of a cake and, for the very artistic, some of the techniques may be used in other areas of cookery.

All embroidery uses some basic techniques that include the dot, line, curve and leaf. A wide range of embroidery is achieved by using a number of these techniques to duplicate what is usually part of textile decorations. The basic techniques of embroidery are discussed on the following pages. There is also a selection of textile stitches that have not been used in cake decorating before (see New Embroidery Designs, pp. 47–51, and colour plates throughout this book).

Dots

This most humble decoration can be found on almost all decorated cakes. Dots can be piped in a variety of sizes, and they can be smooth and round or piped as a peak dot to achieve particular effects.

Method

1 Use an icing bag fitted with a No. 00 icing tube and fill it with soft-peak royal icing (see p. 99).

2 Hold the tip close to the surface where the dot is required. Press the end of the bag and allow the icing to flow until a dot of the required size has been formed. Release the pressure but hold the tip of the tube within the dot of icing. If the dot is to be quite large, a circular motion will help distribute the icing so that a nice round dot can be formed.

3 Withdraw the tip of the tube and you should be left with a soft rounded dot. Continue to pipe dots as required until you gain confidence. Practise small, medium and large dots by using the same technique.

Peak Dots

Method

Repeat steps 1 and 2 as above. However, for peak dots, the tip of the tube must be withdrawn while pressure is still applied. In other words the icing is still being released from the tube as it is withdrawn so that it forms a short line or peak as the dot is completed. These dots are required when small birds are piped or for other particular effects such as French Knots (see p. 49).

Note that if longer stiff peaks are required, it may be necessary to use a slightly firmer icing.

Lines

Lines of varying lengths are used for printing, lattice work, or, of course, in extension work. Lines may be thin or thick. A star tube will create a linear effect.

Method

1 Use a bag with a tube as you did for the Dots. Follow the same procedure but this time, instead of allowing the icing to thicken, begin to lift the tube away from the work area once the icing has become attached.

2 Draw the tube up and away from the work in the direction where the line is required. Continue to press the icing while this is done otherwise the strand will break. The icing strand will still be suspended in mid-air at this stage.

3 Drop the line when the desired length has been drawn from the tube. Allow the tip of the tube to touch at the finishing point and then draw it away with a clean, quick sweep. Practise several of these. Remember that the same technique may be used with a star tube also.

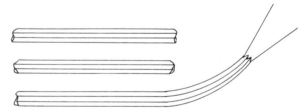

Curves

Curves can be small or large depending on the need. Small curves form part of cursive writing while the larger ones can be stems, branches or scrolls.

Method

1 Fill an icing bag as you did for Dots, step 1. Commence as for a dot but this time draw the tube in the direction of the required curve. The tip of the tube should be as close as possible to the work so that the icing will fall where it is required. To do this, allow the left hand to support the right. Practise small curves first because they are easier than the larger ones.

2   Longer curves are made in the same way as above. Small pin holes may be used as a guide to ensure the curves are piped exactly where they are required. These holes can be your resting spots. Any joins may be smoothed by brushing with a damp brush.

Scallops

These are curves also, but since the technique used is different it is best to treat them separately.

Method

1   Scallops are usually required on the side of a cake, as, for example, the base of extension work. Work out how many scallops are required and also their depth. Mark your cake accordingly with a pin hole at the beginning, end, and lowest part of each scallop.

2   Fill an icing bag as you did for Dots, step 1. The technique used will be similar to that used for the Lines. Commence by forming the beginning of a dot at the top, left-hand point of the scallop. Once the icing has been attached at this point continue to press the bag so that a nice long strand of icing is drawn. Continue to press until the strand drawn is long enough to reach across to the other top point of the scallop. Move your tube across to this point slowly. Although gravity will pull your thread

down in an arch, ensure that the thread is long enough to touch the base curve of the scallop.

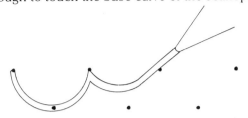

3   Once the thread is long enough to reach across to the top, right-hand point of the scallop and it is also deep enough to touch the base curve, allow it to adhere to the cake by letting the tube touch the top, right-hand point. The scallop will fall against the side of the cake. Scallops made in this way will be perfectly smooth and even. Continue until all the required curves have been formed.

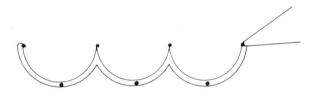

Note that if a scallop requires several layers as in extension work, each layer must be exactly the same size. They will then fall neatly one on top of the other. If there are any spaces between each scallop strand, brush these down with a damp brush.

Leaves

There are three basic leaf designs: the fully closed leaf known as the drag leaf; the outline leaf; and the small outline daisy leaf which appears as an open drag leaf. All of these leaves may be used in a variety of ways for different effects.

Drag Leaves

Method

Fill an icing bag and pipe a large, fat dot. Maintain the pressure and slowly draw along in the required direction. Release the pressure but continue to move in the same direction. Pull away cleanly when you have the required length.

Smaller or larger leaves can be made by extending or reducing the drag stage. Do not forget to maintain the pressure during the middle stage of the leaf otherwise a dot with a tail will be formed instead of a leaf.

These leaves may be arranged along curved stems or in clusters to form daisies or other flowers. They may also be presented with the rounded part at the centre or to the outside. Each method produces different effects.

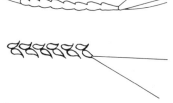

Drag leaves can also be piped at the base of a cake between the base and the board. This continuous line is often called beading or a running dot line. Different effects can be achieved by enlarging or reducing the length and width of the leaf. Of course it is also possible to pipe these lines of leaves in places other than the base of a cake. When such lines are piped with the leaves at right angles to each other a herringbone effect is achieved.

Outline Leaves

As the name suggests, these are the outlines of a leaf or leaf-shaped petals. Leaves can be large or small depending on your particular needs. It is also possible to use an outline technique for sprays or small pictures.

Method

1 Mark out a design on the cake so that your leaves will look natural. If you can do this work freehand, it will have a more natural appearance. However, if a guide is required, mark the beginning and end of each leaf with a series of pin holes.

2 Prepare an icing bag as you did for Dots, step 1 (see p. 44) and commence in the same way. Maintain the pressure and follow one side of the leaf pattern, then stop and draw the tip of the tube away. Repeat the same on the other side to form the second half of the leaf. If a more complex leaf is required, it may be necessary to stop more than once while piping each half.

3 Return to the centre of the leaf and pipe small vein lines where required.

Daisy Leaves

These leaves are very versatile. They can be used in the same ways as the drag leaf, although they are not as effective at the base of a cake.

Method

Prepare an icing bag as you did for Dots, step 1 (see p. 44) and commence in the same way. Use the same technique as for Curves (see pp. 44–45). Pipe one half, and then return and pipe the second half. If these are to represent daisies, pipe a very short line at one point of the leaf.

Now that the basic techniques have been completed some different and lesser known embroidery designs can be attempted.

Embroidery Application

Method

1 You do not have to be a good artist to be able to transfer embroidery patterns onto a cake. Once the cake has been covered and dried, cut out a strip of greaseproof paper which is as long as the circumference and as wide as the height of the cake. If the cake is square or rectangular, it is possible to use a piece of paper which is only as long and wide as one side face of the cake.

Fold the strip of paper allowing one fold for each pattern required. If a cake is to have four repeating patterns then the paper will be divided into four equal sections.

2 Draw or trace the pattern onto one of these sections. If the pattern is to be continuous around the cake it will fill the full length of the section. If it is to be spaced in the centre only, it will be necessary to have space on either side of the pattern. Once this has been completed refold the paper and then retrace or pinprick the pattern onto the other sections.

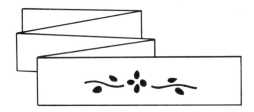

3 Place the strip of paper around the cake and join the two ends together with a piece of tape making sure it does not stick to the cake surface. Place a pin where the first pattern begins, and then pinprick the patterns all around the cake. The first pin will hold the paper in place. Pinpricks should be light so they do not spoil the cake covering. It is not necessary to mark too many holes, just at the start and finish of lines or curves. Leaves and flowers can be treated in the same way. If too many holes are made, all that will appear, when the paper is removed, is a maze of holes which do not make any sense. When piping, place the drawing beside the cake so that you can use it as a guide.

For single sides of cakes, transfer patterns by using the same technique.

New Embroidery Designs

A wide variety of ideas for embroidery can be found in embroidery books, on transfers, and on baby clothes and fancy linen. Laces also offer new ideas for embroidery and piped sugar lace. The following new designs (see Appliqué, Cross Stitch, Eyelet Work, Flooded Embroidery, French Knots, Pulled Thread Work, Satin Stitch, Shadow Stitch, Stem Stitch and Cable Stitch) will provide many different effects for your cakes. Experiment with a variety of coloured icings to widen the range of your work even further.

Appliqué

(see colour plate opposite p. 48)

This form of embroidery combines piping work with the application of small, fine pieces of icing used as an overlay. A number of differently coloured overlays, or pieces of icing which are shaded or marbled, can be used for variety.

Method

1 Draw up one section of the required design including areas suitable for your appliqué pieces.

2 Mark the design onto the cake surface with a pin, taking care to make only very fine holes. Colour small pieces of paste or soft icing according to the colour scheme you want. If any sections are to be shaded, this can be done once the pieces are cut out ready to place on the cake.

3 Use a little petal dust on a dry brush to achieve a shaded effect on any parts of the appliqué which need to be coloured. Note that white appliqué can look very attractive if slightly shaded.

47

4 Roll out the paste or icing, and cut out the required patterns. Pipe a little royal icing on the underside and then place these on the appropriate sections of the design.

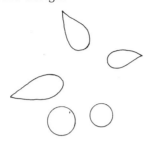

5 Prepare an icing bag as you did for Dots, step 1 (see p. 44). Pipe an outline around each piece being sure to have the strand of icing as close to the edge of the paste as possible. Return and pipe a series of very short lines across the edge of each appliqué piece; these are at right angles to the outline.

6 Finally finish off the work by piping stems, dots, and any other finishing touches you require.

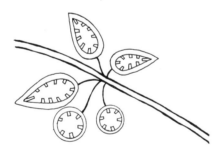

Cross Stitch

(see colour plate opposite p. 32)

This stitch can be piped in monotone or in colours. Stitches can be large or small depending on the design and on the size of the cake.

Method

1 Cross stitch designs are very easy to draw when graph paper is used. Design the required pattern by drawing it onto a piece of tracing paper. Select a piece of graph paper to suit your design: small

squares for small designs and so on. Lay the drawing on the graph paper and cover with a fresh sheet of tracing paper. Cross out the squares so that the pattern is transposed into cross stitch.

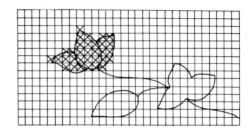

2 Transfer the pattern onto the cake surface with the aid of pin holes and then commence your piping. Remember that many of these patterns look quite effective if they are piped in the same colour so it may be a good idea to begin with a single-tone design.

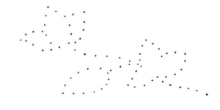

3 Return to pipe any dots, or other sections which would look best in another stitch and then repeat the pattern around the rest of the cake.

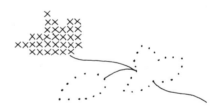

Eyelet Work

(see left colour plate between pp. 72–73)

This work is sometimes called cut-out work. The icing surface needs to be indented so that the

The simple arrangement on this cake consists of autumnal foliage and fruits, while the embroidery design imitates variegated appliqué work. The shape is a classical oval form, with a small section removed to create a depression at the focal point where the arrangement has been placed. (Instructions: Colours and Colouring Techniques, p. 11; Cake Shapes, p. 15; Appliqué, p. 47; Cable Stitch, p. 51; Moulded Fruits, p. 55; Foliage, p. 63; Ribbons, p. 82; Cake Designs, p. 101.)

ABOVE: Harvesting is the time for reaping the fruits of one's labour so this is a perfect cake to celebrate a retirement. The embroidery work on the sides imitates pulled thread work. The serviette ring is decorated with variegated ivy leaves. (Instructions: Pulled Thread Work, p. 50; Stem Stitch, p. 51; Floodwork, p. 54; Floodwork Colouring, p. 55; Ivy Leaves, p. 64; Serviette Rings, p. 67; Cake Designs, p. 102.)

OPPOSITE: A cake in the shape of a ginger jar ornamented with very fragile chrysanthemums creates an effect similar to decorated porcelain. A tall, sharp wooden spike is attached to the board and runs through the middle of the cake to keep it stable. (Instructions: Colours and Colouring Techniques, p. 11; Cakes Shapes, p. 15; Chrysanthemum, p. 60.)

threads of piped icing have space to stand above the depressed surface. It is not necessary to over-pipe the bars and outlines, so single strands will suffice. Pretty effects can be achieved by brushing a little petal dust in the indented areas to highlight the bars and strands piped across the surface.

Method

1 Draw one section of the design and then transfer this onto the cake surface. Once marked, use a small balling tool to indent the relevant sections but be careful not to damage the other areas. This part of the work should be done as soon as possible after the cake icing has set because the firmer the surface the more difficult it will be. Note that when you do eyelet work, confine the indented areas to small narrow sections. Ridges will be apparent in larger work.

2 Brush a little petal dust onto the indented surfaces. Then pipe outlines where required.

Painted autumn scenes have great versatility. This country lane with its soft, hazy gold and green tones has a tranquil beauty which makes it ideal for many celebrations. The knife has been decorated with maple leaves. (Instructions: Colours and Colouring Techniques, p. 11; Embroidery, p. 43; Floodwork, p. 54; Floodwork Colouring, p. 55; Foliage, p. 63; Cake Designs, p. 103.)

3 Pipe a series of parallel lines between the sides of each section of indented icing. These lines represent the buttonholed bars which are embroidered in this sort of work.

4 Return and pipe any other embroidery which may be required to complete the design.

Flooded Embroidery

This work is done in the same way as floodwork except that usually the pictures are much smaller. They may be small sprays of flowers or small figures or people. Outlines can be piped in white or coloured icing. The flooding icing should be much firmer than that for floodwork. Use a brush to move the icing to the required sections. If the cake surface is completely dry, tilt the cake a little to enable the work to be done with a minimum of fuss. Follow the instructions given for Floodwork (see pp. 54–55).

French Knots

(see colour plate opposite p. 88)

This work is an adapted version since the icing looks best if the dots have a peak.

Method

Prepare an icing bag. Pipe a dot but, before pulling the tip of the tube away from the work, pipe the outline of a small circle and then pull up quickly leaving a peak dot which is enclosed by a circle. French knots are usually used in the centre of flowers.

Pulled Thread Work

(see right colour plate between pp. 48–49)

Once again the piped version is an adaptation. When this technique is used on fabric, a number of threads are pulled away from the material which is then stitched to form a series of small even holes.

Method

1 Draw up one section of the required pattern and then transfer it onto the cake surface.

2 Use an outline embroidery and any other combinations to complete the pattern. Use a cocktail stick or something similar to make a hole pattern in the areas where you want the pulled thread effect. These holes should be placed between each of the holes in the previous row giving a brickwork effect.

3 Pipe lines between the rows of holes like the lines of mortar between bricks. These will form small squares around each hole.

Petal dust can be brushed into these holes if you want a colour highlight but this should be done prior to piping the final lines.

Satin Stitch

(see colour plate opposite p. 80)

There are several variations of this stitch which can be used for piped embroidery.

Method

1 Draw up one section of the design you want and then transfer this onto the cake. Embroider all areas which require other techniques first.

2 For plain satin stitch, pipe a series of lines next to each other. Be sure not to leave any space between them. Continue until the area to be decorated has been filled. These lines can be piped in a coloured icing.

3 Long and short satin stitch can be piped as an alternative to the above method. Commence at the outer edge of the work; in the case of the flower below, start from the edge of the petal and work inwards. Pipe a series of alternate short and long lines. This technique lends itself to colour variation. For instance, the outer section can be piped in dark tones and graduated to very pale tones in the centre.

4 For flat or fishbone stitch pipe the area with short, half-width lines. The flat work has short, parallel lines while the fishbone stitch has the lines piped at a slant to give an angled effect.

Shadow Stitch

(see colour plate opposite p. 88)

This work is very soft and pale so it is suitable for wedding colour schemes or for a baby's christening cake.

Method

1 Draw one section of the required pattern and then transfer this onto the cake surface. Embroider all the areas which require other piping techniques.

2 Pipe a series of very fine, short lines around the outer edge of the work; in the case of the flower below, start from the edge of the petal and work inwards. Pipe a series of alternate short and long lines. This technique lends itself to colour variation. For instance, the outer section can be piped in dark tones and graduated to very pale tones in the centre.

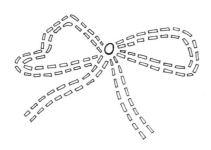

3 Once all of the outlines have been completed, the enclosed areas can be coloured. Plan your colour scheme and then lightly brush the enclosed areas with dry petal dust. This colouring should be very soft with perhaps a little grading in tones.

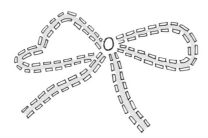

Stem Stitch

(see colour plate opposite p. 80)

Stem stitch is one of the most basic embroidery stitches. This work consists of a series of very short, slightly slanted lines along stems or other outlines.

Method

1 Draw one section of the required pattern and transfer this onto the cake surface. Embroider all the areas which require other piping techniques.

2 Pipe a series of short-angled lines where you have chosen to use stem stitch. These lines can be slightly curved, as they are on fabric. The shorter the stitches, the more effective this work will be.

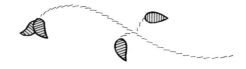

Cable stitch

(see colour plate opposite p. 48)

Method

1 Draw one section of the required design and transfer this onto the cake surface.

2 Pipe a series of short lines where cable stitch is required. Note that there should be a small space between each line. Return and pipe another row of short, small-spaced lines directly below the first row, making sure that the lines are below the spaces of the first row.

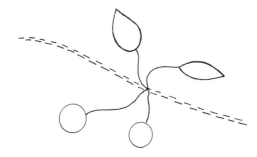

Lace

Fine, dainty sugar lace gives a cake a soft, elegant touch. It can be used in conjunction with extension work, with embroidery or on its own. Lace is piped in small, individual pieces which are then attached to a cake: they may be placed in rows, scallops or other decorative shapes. Flower arrangements on the top of a cake can be surrounded by a pretty lace design.

There are many traditional lace designs which have become classics because of their versatility and beauty. Others are an obvious choice for particular occasions: hearts for engagements and weddings, bells for weddings and Christmas.

New designs can easily be created as long as a few points are taken into consideration. For best results, lace pieces should be fine and dainty. Care should be taken not to create pieces which are too long or wide because these are sometimes difficult to use. If multi-coloured pieces are to be used, do not make the bottom lace the same colour as the board (you will lose the definition of the bottom lace if there is no colour contrast). The outer edges of the lace should sit comfortably beside another similar piece, otherwise they will not be effective when arranged. If the lace is to be placed in very deep scallops, wide pieces of lace can cause problems at the top and curve of the scallops.

Fine print fabrics, old lace pieces or even patterns on wrapping paper can provide ideas for new designs. Exact patterns need not be copied, simply select the suitable sections which will provide a theme for your work. Small outline drawings of the flowers within a spray also make ideal lace or embroidery patterns.

Method

1 Take a piece of imperial graph paper and draw a selection of lace designs in rows of ten. Metric graph paper can cause problems because the small squares are far too close together to allow for the width of your icing lines. The lines may merge and your lace will not have fine holes. Don't use more than four or five small squares for either the width or the length of your lace pieces. There are some designs which do require more length but these should not be attempted until you have had some practice.

2 Use a firm board or several thicknesses of cardboard as a base for your work. Place the graph paper on this. Cut a sheet of waxed paper which is larger than the graph paper and place it over the top. Be sure the shiny surface faces up, so that when the lace pieces are removed they will lift off easily. Pin down the four corners of the waxed paper being sure to leave the graph paper free. In this way, as each row of lace is piped, the paper can be pulled down a little allowing you to pipe further rows of the same design.

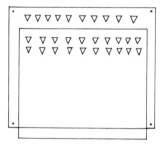

3 Make some royal icing to a soft-peak consistency (see p. 99). It is recommended that you sift the icing sugar three times and whip the egg white when making icing for lace or extension work. Fit a No. 00 or a No. 000 tube to an icing bag and fill. Hold the tube over a damp cloth and press the bag until the icing is flowing freely, which makes this work much easier.

4 Commence piping the lace pieces from left to right. This will enable you to follow the design more easily. Pipe the lace in complete sweeps so that there is a minimum of joins. If, for example, the design has several rows, pipe the pieces row by row. Do not stop in the middle of the row. If the design is not in rows, it may be better to pipe it one half at a time. Always moisten the joins with a slightly damp brush and take care that all strands of icing are joined together. If there are single dots, or a flower in the centre which does not join some other part, this section will remain on the paper when the piece is removed.

5 Once a complete row has been piped, pull the graph paper down a little and repeat the process. This will ensure the lace is produced in rows of ten. These sheets of paper can be rolled lightly and then stored in a perspex-covered box (this will mean that you won't have to open the box and risk damage to the pieces). Lace can be stored in this way for many months. Note that if lace is stored for a year or two it may discolour or become crystalline.

6 Calculate the number of lace pieces you require. This can be done by measuring the circumference of the cake and dividing it by the width of the lace piece. It is important, however, to make many extra pieces because they are so fragile that breakages are to be expected.

Attaching Lace

Method

1 Mark out the area where the lace is to be placed. This can be done by running the tip of a pin along the line or scallop. A fine white mark will be left on the surface of the cake.

2 Attach the lace to the cake with short, fine lines of icing or, if the design is suitable, two or three dots. Remove the lace piece from the waxed paper by bending the paper slightly. Lean the top, wider part of the lace against the line or dots. Hold the piece for a few seconds until the icing begins to set. Slant the piece as required, before applying the next one. Lace should be placed on a cake at a 45-degree angle. Remember to allow some space between lace pieces so that the outer curves do not break against each other.

Multi-tone Lace

Multi-tone lace can be made by using two or three tubes of differently coloured icing. Some patterns look very attractive done in this way. For example, holly leaves and red berries look attractive on a Christmas cake. Gold or silver dots can also be added to give variety to the lace.

Flooded Lace

Small, flooded sections can be incorporated in lace for particular effects.

Method

Once the pieces have been made, small sections can be filled with a watered-down icing. This icing should not be too moist because the strength of the lines will deteriorate. Brush the icing into the required sections and then allow the lace to dry again. Allow 24 hours drying before removing from the paper. Apply these pieces in the same way as other varieties of lace.

Flower Lace

A flower effect can be created by placing two rows of lace together. It will be necessary, however, to design lace pieces which look like the petals of a flower.

Method

Pipe the lace pieces and then allow them to dry thoroughly. Arrange the pieces in pairs above and below each other so that each pair forms a flower. The top row will slant up while the bottom row will need to slant down.

Floodwork

The art of making sugar-painted pictures is called floodwork. This term refers to all painting methods, including the occasional work which is painted directly onto the cake surface, without the preliminary build-up of icing.

Floodwork is a particularly suitable medium for personalising a cake. Pictures can be copied from birthday cards, be of favourite places or hobbies, or they can be reproductions of such things as wedding invitations. Favourite colours and the use of multiple techniques can also add that special, personal touch. This is a truly versatile medium.

Floodwork can be done on three surfaces: straight onto the surface of a dry, iced cake; onto waxed paper; or onto a dry plaque made from gum paste or soft icing. To apply the picture to the surface it is necessary to trace the drawing and then turn the tracing upside down and re-draw over the back of the lines. Place the drawing onto the surface to be treated and then re-trace. Be sure to have the picture right side up (an inverted drawing makes painting difficult). A good artist may draw freehand straight onto the cake, using a fine pencil or a long-handled pin. If a pin is used, scratch a very fine line onto the surface. If a pencil is used be careful not to smudge or make mistakes since these lines will be hard to disguise or erase.

Once the drawing has been completed there are three methods which can be used.

Methods

1 The drawing can be flooded in with a softened royal icing. Royal icing can be made thinner with water, extra egg white or lemon juice; all are equally satisfactory. Once watered down, the consistency of the icing should be about the same as thickened cream before it is whipped. If the icing is to be used on the side of a cake, or on areas which are to give a built-up effect, it may be necessary to have the icing much thicker. Remember that if very small, fine areas are to be covered, a thinner icing will brush on smoothly without leaving marks. Bulges and ripples need thicker icing with softer icing brushed up to, or over, it so that these bulges can be retained.

2 Prior to filling, the outlines can be piped over in royal icing. If working with this method, be sure to have the outlines as smooth as possible. Joins and ripples should be moistened with a damp brush.

The outlines can be piped in white or coloured icing, depending on the design and the required effect. When using coloured icing, be sure to mix enough royal icing to outline the entire picture in order to avoid colour-matching problems.

3 Alternatively fill in the picture without any outlines at all. Whether outlining or not, use either a paint brush, or a piping bag, to fill in the design. If a large area is to be covered it may be easier to use a combination of the two techniques.

You can create three-dimensional effects by re-flooding the same areas several times to build up a layer effect. Work out a suitable pattern for this build-up, ensuring that items closest to the foreground have several layers while those in the background have fewer so that they appear to recede. Free-standing items can also be made using the floodwork technique. Make these by flooding onto waxed paper, allowing to dry thoroughly, and then re-flooding on the back and allowing to dry once again.

The icing used for flooding can be white or coloured. When using several different colours for the sections of a picture, allow each to dry completely before commencing on the next colour. Another method is to work on alternate areas in order to avoid colour seepage while sections are still drying. If very dark colours such as brown or navy are required, it is best to use powder colours. Be very careful with dark icing because of the risk of seeping, discolouring and staining. Shading can be done when a picture is completely dry regardless of whether coloured or white icing has been used for filling. Note, however, that dark shades cannot be made lighter.

If frills or flounces are to be added to part of a flooded picture, such as the petticoat showing under a skirt, make the Simple Frill as described on p. 26, and then apply it to the underskirt after the drawing has been traced onto the cake. Proceed with the flooding in the usual manner but ensure that the join is covered. The result will be a very attractive, three-dimensional effect. Piped flowers or leaves can also be incorporated into these pictures to give more detail to the work.

Scenes such as landscapes can be partially flooded and the more distant features can be painted straight onto the cake surface. This can be done freehand or by using a traced drawing. With the advent of petal dusts and pastels, these backgrounds can be made to look realistically soft and hazy. This same method can be used for the background when more traditional figures have been flooded. Lightly brush the coloured powder onto the surface of the cake. Paint several colours into areas such as distant hills or foreground grass. Once these colours have been brushed, return with a little cornflour on the brush and work all over the painted area so the colours blend and merge. Remember that colours require contrasts so dark shades should be against lighter tones.

Wait until all flooded areas are completely dry before attempting any shadowing. Details such as the print design on a dress or shirt, the folds of a skirt, or the shadows in a landscape should all be slightly understated. Although prints may be in a check or striped design, they do not appear uniform when being worn. Spots and floral patterns also vary depending on intensity of light. Use a pale caramel instead of black for details or else a deeper shade of the same colour. Features on faces can be lightly brushed on with a cotton bud. Eyes and mouth should be painted in a series of small dots or lines rather than one broad stroke which can be too harsh. Remember that once a colour has been applied it is very difficult to remove or lighten. If a mistake has been made it is sometimes possible to re-flood that area and then colour it again. If you are careful the re-flooded area can show through the previously applied colour so that it appears in a lighter tone. Always work with a cloth beside the work so that any excess colour can be wiped off the brush prior to painting.

It is possible to do floodwork onto a suitably shaped plaque and then place it on a cake. Such an item could be arranged with other sugar ornaments for a three-dimensional effect.

Floodwork Colouring

Floodwork is treated in much the same way as colouring on paper. Icings can be coloured first and then, when the surface has dried, have highlights added by colouring with a brush. Another method is to flood in white icing and then colour as required. Remember that grainy, porous surfaces absorb too much colour so it is best to avoid these.

When painting over flooded surfaces, any type of colour can be used. Liquid colours can give both soft and deep tones while powders and pastels usually give soft effects. Paste colours are useful for very fine details. It is not necessary to use only the one type of colour. Combinations of all types can be used according to need. As with flower colouring, methylated spirits is used for applying and diluting colours.

Moulded Fruits

Moulded fruits are generally made from marzipan. Depending on size, they are usually presented in clusters, or in containers such as a basket, on a cake. The larger fruits are made for gift giving so these tend to be presented in pretty boxes. The following fruits have been chosen because they offer more possibilities for natural presentation. Stems have been used for all of the fruits presented on the cakes within this book.

Crab Apples

(see colour plate opposite p. 48)

Method

1 Cut several pieces of fine cotton-covered wire to suitable lengths for the stems and make a small hook at one end of each piece.

2 Take a small piece of paste and work this between your hands forming a small ball about 1.5 cm in diameter. Insert the tip of a skewer at the top and bottom of this ball to indent the area for the stem and base of the fruit. Moisten the hooked end of a piece of cotton-covered wire and insert this into one of the indentations. Ensure the wire is attached securely so that it will not fall out. Use a skewer or other suitable tool and hollow out a small area around the stem. Shape the base of the fruit so that it becomes a little narrower. Once completed drop the fruit into a bowl of cornflour until it is dry. This ensures pieces dry with an attractive, rounded appearance rather than becoming flat.

Grapes

(see colour plate opposite p. 64)

Grapes can be made in the same way as the apples except that they should be shaped in a soft drop or oval shape. Attach stems to each grape and then dry in the usual way. Present these in clusters so that they resemble real grapes.

Acorns

(see colour plate opposite p. 48)

Although not a traditional moulded fruit, acorns

55

can make beautiful decorations for an autumn cake.

Method

1 Take several pieces of fine cotton-covered wire and make a small hook at one end of each piece.

2 Take a piece of paste and mould this to a long cylindrical shape about 1–2 cm in length and 8–12 mm in width. Moisten the hooked end of a piece of wire and insert this into one end of the paste.

3 Press and squeeze the join so the wire will remain securely attached. Run the top third of the paste over a fine grater to indent a pattern on the top part of the acorn. Use a blunt knife or other suitable tool to form a line or ridge a third of the way down the acorn, just below the patterned area. Mould the base to make it a little narrower just as a real acorn appears. When complete, drop the acorn into a container of cornflour until it is dry.

Moulded Toys

Teddy Bears

(see right colour plate between pp. 88–89)

Sugar replicas of these much loved toys can add a little magic to any child's cake.

Method

1 Take a piece of paste which is large enough to make a fat, squat sausage 8 cm in length and 4–5 cm in width.

2 Use a small pair of scissors to cut a pair of legs from the base of this paste. These should be 3–4 cm in length. Legs are formed by cutting down the middle of the paste.

3 Work the top of the paste to form a head. The head forms part of the whole piece, and should be about 2 cm in height.

4 Use the scissors once again to cut a pair of arms just below the head.

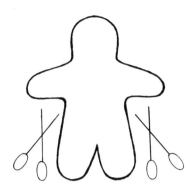

5 If any of these features appear to be too small, knead a little extra paste into them. Use your tools or a fine skewer to indent lines and make features on the teddy. Squeeze out a small section at the top of the head to the left and right to represent ears. Push down a little where the eyes are to be and pull out a little paste just below these to represent the snout.

6 Use a blunt needle to mark out stitch lines if your teddy is to have these or mark it with creases or folds. When complete, set it aside in a container of cornflour until it has dried. Colour and paint in the features.

Blocks

(see right colour plate between pp. 88–89)

You can make blocks with small pieces of paste or icing cut into cubes. Use a sharp knife so the lines remain clean and crisp. Place these in cornflour until they have dried and then colour them as required.

Use your imagination to produce other suitable toys and animals for young children's cakes.

Moulded Flowers

Camellia

(see left colour plate between pp. 64–65)

This very popular plant has many varieties, all of which have magnificent flowers (flowering season depends on the species). Although they are all beautiful, many of the flowers are not suitable for cake decorating since they are far too large. Instructions are given here for a particularly elegant and small variety. The flowers can be white or the palest pink, so they would be an ideal choice for a wedding or engagement cake. Once again it is best to have a real sample to copy from when making these.

Flower

Classed as a formal double, the camellia presented here has many layers of petals evenly placed around the centre. No stamens are visible.

Method

1 Take a ball of paste which is about 5 mm in diameter. Roll the paste between the fingers to form a short sausage shape. Press and flatten this so that a long narrow piece is formed, about 2 cm in length and 7 mm in width. Cut this in half down the centre and then, using a balling tool, press the inside of each of these two petals so that they become concave. Set these aside to dry in a shallow patty tin.

2 Use a small rose cutter for the next row of petals or, if preferred, make a cutter or template using the pattern below. Take a small piece of paste and roll it out as thinly as possible. Cut out five petals and ball the inside of these to give them a soft, rounded curve. The centre top part of the petals should be pinched very lightly, just enough

to give a slight point in the centre. Set these aside to dry in a shallow patty tin.

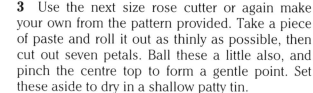

3 Use the next size rose cutter or again make your own from the pattern provided. Take a piece of paste and roll it out as thinly as possible, then cut out seven petals. Ball these a little also, and pinch the centre top to form a gentle point. Set these aside to dry in a shallow patty tin.

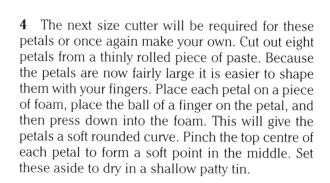

4 The next size cutter will be required for these petals or once again make your own. Cut out eight petals from a thinly rolled piece of paste. Because the petals are now fairly large it is easier to shape them with your fingers. Place each petal on a piece of foam, place the ball of a finger on the petal, and then press down into the foam. This will give the petals a soft rounded curve. Pinch the top centre of each petal to form a soft point in the middle. Set these aside to dry in a shallow patty tin.

5 The final layer of petals consists of six rounded petals. Roll out another piece of paste large enough to have six small circles cut out of it. Any small round cutter will do for this, or else use a bottle top no larger than 2–2.5 cm in diameter.

These petals can be curved by using the same method described in step 4 above. Set these aside to dry in a shallow patty tin.

6 Assemble the flower on a piece of foil which has been shaped to a soft curve by pressing it into a shallow patty tin. The flower may be assembled either from the centre to the outside or from the outside into the middle. Pipe a large dot of royal icing in the centre of the foil and then commence arranging the petals.

Arrange the centre petals so that they are upright with the tips slanting towards each other. Arrange the petals row by row (they do not have to overlap) ensuring that the flower has a pleasing shape and looks realistic. Add more icing as required. Be sure to arrange the petals in rows according to size (smaller petals at the centre), then set the flower aside to dry.

Calyx

The calyx on camellias does not have the usual pointed sepals. They are rounded, rather like smaller green petals.

Method

1 Take a piece of paste which is 1–1.5 cm in diameter and form it into a small dome. Moisten the flat part of the dome and gently press it onto the back of a dry, completed flower. It is advisable to

place the flower onto a piece of cotton wool so that the pressure will not cause it to break. Insert into the centre of the dome the hooked end of a 15 cm piece of medium or heavy cotton-covered wire, then pinch and squeeze to secure the wire.

2 Roll out a piece of paste as thinly as possible and then cut out five small circular sepals. A small bottle top can be used as an alternative to a cutter but be sure it is no larger than 1–1.5 cm in diameter. Squeeze each sepal so that the cutting edge is softened. Moisten the sepals and lay them over the dome. The sepals should overlap as they rotate. Be sure that the base of each sepal is right up against the wire. The calyx thus formed will spread from the edge of the wire, over the dome and partly onto the base of the flower petals. Once completed, set aside to dry thoroughly before colouring.

Leaf

Camellia leaves are strikingly dark and glossy. They are often quite large and also very strong. It is suggested that these be made in a smaller version and that colouring be adjusted to complement your colour scheme because sometimes very dark leaves can look too heavy.

Method

As the real camellia leaves are so strong they may be used to make your sugar ones. Collect several of the smallest leaves available. Take a piece of paste

59

and roll it out so that it is very thin at one end and slightly thicker at the other. Place a piece of paste on the underside of a leaf that has been dusted with cornflour. Press the paste so that the veins are indented into it. Gently tear away the excess paste as it is pulled up at the outer edges. This process can be done on a plastic leaf if the real product is not available. As the paste is removed from the edges, press against the rim of the leaf so that the serrations are also pressed into the paste. Insert the moistened, hooked end of a 15 cm piece of medium cotton-covered wire. Bend and curve the leaf and then place it on top of some suitably shaped foil so that it will dry with a realistic curve.

Chrysanthemum

(see left colour plate between pp. 48–49)

These flowers come in a variety of colours and sizes. As they are so time-consuming to make, the following instructions relate to the simplest type of chrysanthemum. As you gain more experience, it will be possible to adapt the method to other more complex varieties.

Flower

A variety of petal sizes will need to be made for this flower. Petals can be made in eight different sizes but no particular number is required for each row.

Method

1 Take a ball of paste which is about 3 mm in diameter. Roll this to a thin sausage and then push a paint brush handle along its length. This will have the twofold effect of flattening and thinning the petal as well as giving it a curved appearance. If the ends look frayed just brush away any excess paste. Be sure the ends are slightly pointed and narrower than the rest of the petal. These petals will be 5–7 mm in length. Make at least four of these petals for each flower.

2 Take a ball of paste which is 4 mm in diameter, then proceed in the same way as above. Be sure that the completed petals are about 1 cm in length. Make eight to ten petals in this way and then set them aside to dry in a shallow patty pan which has been dusted with cornflour.

3 Take a ball of paste which is 5 mm in diameter. Make these petals in the same way as above but widen them a little so that they are increasing in width as well as length. Make ten to twelve petals for this row and then set them aside to dry.

4 Take a ball of paste which is 6 mm in diameter. Roll this out to a thin sausage ensuring that the centre is a little fatter than the ends. Roll the paint brush handle along the length of the paste. Using this method, ensure the petal becomes boat-shaped. When placing these aside to dry, push the top end down a little so that it curves inwards. Petals on this flower can all be gently curved inwards. However, in some varieties the inner petals have a deeper curve than those on the outside.

5 Petals for the fifth row will be about 2 cm in length. Take a ball of paste which is 7 mm in diameter and proceed to make these petals in the same way as above but increase their width as well as the length. Increase the length of the petals for the sixth row to 2–2.5 cm and be sure to make about twelve petals for each of these rows.

6 Rows seven and eight have petals which are made in exactly the same way as the previous ones. Ensure that row seven petals are closer to 3 cm in length while those for the last row should be almost 4 cm in length. The width of the petals will be 5–8 cm in the final rows. Do not forget to ensure the curve becomes gentler for the outer petals also. The suggested number of petals for these two rows is fifteen each.

7 When all the petals are completely dry, the flower can be assembled. Take a piece of aluminium foil about 8 by 8 cm. Place a 1.5 cm circle of firm royal icing in the centre of the foil. This should be about 5 mm in height. It needs to be large enough to securely hold the rows of petals, but if the quantity is too generous it will be visible between the rows and look heavy. Practice will be the best guide for good results.

Commence by inserting the four smallest petals which will form the centre of the flower. Select the next row of dried petals and place these around the centre which you have formed. The number required will vary depending on their width and curve, but be sure to use enough to give the impression of unfurling petals. At this point there should be enough royal icing showing to place the third row of petals. If this is not the case, pipe some royal icing around the outside of the assembled petals and assemble the third row. Subsequent rows of petals do not have to be placed between the previous ones as long as the final flower appears realistic.

8 Arrange the fourth row of petals in much the same way as the previous rows. Be sure to pipe some extra royal icing, then place as many petals as are required.

Continue to assemble the flower in this way until all eight rows have been completed. It may be necessary to return and place an odd petal in any spaces which become apparent as the flower is completed. If this is the case, be sure to pipe some royal icing on the base of the petal before inserting it into position. Remember it may be necessary to vary the size of these flowers so some may have fewer rows of petals. If a cup-shaped flower is required, the foil may be shaped accordingly in a shallow patty tin. Allow the flowers to dry for at least 24 hours before adding their calyxes.

Buds

The larger buds are made in the same way as the flower. Be sure to make your buds in varying sizes so that the final spray can look realistic.

Method

1 To make petals for the buds, follow the flower-making instructions as far as step 4, making sure that you give your petals a nice deep curve as this helps to make a realistic looking bud.

2 When all the petals are completely dry, the bud can be assembled. Take a piece of aluminium foil about 8 by 8 cm and place this in a shallow patty tin to give it a curved shape. Place a 1.5 cm circle of firm royal icing in the centre of the foil. This should be about 5 mm in height; it needs to be large enough to securely hold the rows of petals.

3 Commence by inserting the four smallest petals that will form the centre of the bud, making sure that you place them close together. Attach the next row of petals around the centre which you have formed. If you do not want the bud to be too large use fewer petals but be sure to have them slanted inwards to give an unfurling effect. Assemble the next two rows in the same way adding more royal icing as required. Set aside to dry.

Calyx

These flowers look more realistic when assembled with calyxes. Since the final flower will be quite heavy, it may be desirable to use a heavy gauge wire for best support. Note that because these flowers are so fragile you may decide to use them without calyxes.

Method

1 Take a ball of paste which is about 1–1.5 cm in diameter. Form this into a fat, shallow cone shape. Take a piece of cotton-covered wire which is about 15 cm in length and form a small hook at one end. Moisten this end being sure to shake off any excess water. Insert into the lower part of the cone and pinch to attach it securely.

2 Using either a suitable balling tool or the handle of a brush, hollow out the cone to form a cup about 1.5 cm in diameter. Divide the top of the cup into several 5 mm deep sections by cutting with a fine pair of scissors. It will not be possible to make all the sepals which this flower has in its natural state, but be sure to make as many as possible without them looking too small. Once the divisions have been made, they can then be shaped by hand. Squeeze and pinch each sepal to the required shape.

3 The calyx is now ready to attach to the flower. Remove the flower from the foil and place it on a bed of cotton wool. Moisten the inside of the calyx with water and then gently press onto the back of the flower. Set aside to dry thoroughly before colouring. The calyx can also be attached by piping some royal icing on the inside rather than using the water. If the back of the flower is untidy, it may be necessary to file down any excess icing or, in severe cases, to use a larger calyx.

Leaf

Method

Roll out some paste as thinly as possible. Leave it a little thicker at the end where the stem is to be. Using one of the templates, cut out the required shape. Insert the hooked end of a moistened wire to form the stem and squeeze and pinch to attach it securely. Use the handle of a paint brush to lightly frill some of the edges to give a natural effect and then set aside to dry.

 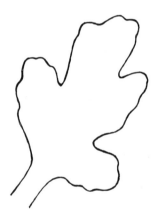

Nerine

(see left colour plate between pp. 64–65)

These beautiful spider-like flowers are very popular for bridal bouquets. The most popular colours are white and the various shades of pink. However, they are also available in red, orange and yellow. This wide colour range makes them ideal flowers for many occasions. No buds or leaves are made for this flower as they are not very attractive and are never used in floral arrangements.

Flower

Before completion each petal of the nerine is frilled to help achieve the spidery look.

Method

1 Take a 12–15 cm piece of fine or medium cotton-covered wire and make a small hook at one end. Take a ball of paste which is about 1.5 cm in diameter and roll this between the fingers to form a large teardrop which is 2 cm in length. Moisten the hooked end of the wire and insert it into the point of the teardrop. Squeeze and pinch the base to secure it firmly.

2 Using the handle of a paint brush or any other suitable tool hollow out the paste to form a large hollow cone which is about 2.5–3 cm in length and about the same in width. To hollow the paste, use a rotating motion being sure to rotate both the paste and the tool. Press firmly while rotating to thin out the paste. Once the cone is large enough it is possible to complete the process by using the fingers to squeeze the sides. When making a large cone this method gives better results. The base of the cone does not need to be hollowed.

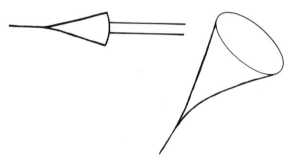

3 Using a pair of fine-bladed scissors, cut the cone into six equal-sized petals. It is easiest to first divide the cone in half and then each half can be cut into three petals. The depth of these divisions should be 1.5–2 cm. Each petal will also need to be trimmed because it should be narrow with a curved tip. Cut away a small triangular piece of paste from each side of the petal to remove any excess paste. Remember that these petals are only 5 mm in width.

4 Place the flower onto a piece of rubber so that each petal can be frilled. It is necessary to frill the outer 2 mm of each edge of the petals. This will give the impression of a fatter line running down the centre. This frilling procedure is very delicate because once the petals have been thinned out they are very fragile. Be careful not to allow the petals to adhere to the rubber during this part of the work. Dust the rubber surface with cornflour to avoid this problem. When completed, bend each petal down and under, away from the centre of the flower.

5 Take several stamens with large heads and curve the full length of the cottons by running them between the fingers. Cut them to the same length as the flower, moisten the cut ends and insert into the base of the flower, using a pair of tweezers. If some of the stamens will not adhere to the flower, it may be necessary to wait until the flower is dry and then pipe a little royal icing into the base. Use a minimum amount because too much can make the flower look unrealistic and heavy. Set the flower aside in an upturned egg carton until it is thoroughly dry.

Calyx

Unlike most flowers, the nerine does not have a calyx with individual sepals. Its calyx is like a knob or knuckle attached to the base of the flower.

Method

Take a ball of paste which is 3–4 mm in diameter and roll this between the fingers to form a ball with a flat top. Use the base of a paint brush handle to indent a shallow curve in the top of the paste and squeeze the base to give it a slight point. Moisten the inside of this with a little water and then insert the end of the wire which is attached to the flower. Pull the wire through the calyx and draw the paste up to the base of the flower. Push gently so the calyx can adhere and then squeeze and pinch to ensure the join is neat and smooth. Set aside to dry thoroughly before colouring.

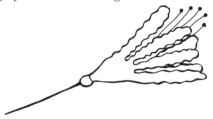

Foliage

Nature provides a vast array of foliage to accompany her glorious jewels. Leaves in a multitude of shapes and sizes, as well as a great diversity of colour, appear during autumn. Although cakes are often presented with a floral arrangement, many are not accompanied by a flattering display of foliage. Whether dark, light or in between, leaves provide a wonderful contrast to delicate flowers. There is no excuse for omitting foliage on your cakes.

There are leaves which make spectacular ornamental decorations. Some of these are the elm, maple and oak leaves (see patterns below and colour plate opposite p. 48). Most leaves are made in the same way as described in the methods below for Grape and Ivy Leaves. Collect sample leaves as a guide. Patterns are included here since it is not always possible to find samples.

Grape Leaves
(see colour plate opposite p. 64)

These leaves are especially beautiful in autumn. The lovely shape, combined with the changing colours, make these suitable for many occasions.

Method

1 Roll out a piece of paste onto a tile or similar surface. Be sure to have one end slightly thicker than the other so there is enough thickness to attach a wire as a stem. Cut out a leaf freehand or use a cutter or template if preferred.

2 Vein the leaf remembering there are five main veins. All the other veins are much lighter so be sure to press gently for these. Gently flute the very outer edges of the paste so that the leaf takes on a more natural appearance. Insert the hooked end of a piece of fine cotton-covered wire into the top part of the leaf and set it aside to dry. Use balls of cotton wool as support for the curves or place the leaf on a plastic replica to give it a better shape.

Ivy Leaves

(see right colour plate between pp. 48–49)

These leaves make an ideal addition to many arrangements since they have such an attractive shape. Presented either in greens or combined with variegated leaves, ivy can be used where other greenery is not suitable. It is suggested that only the small and medium leaves be used because the largest ones can dwarf flowers.

Method

1 Take a piece of paste and roll it out as thinly as possible. Leave it a little thicker at one end. Cut out a leaf shape either freehand or with aid of a cutter. Be sure to place the stem at the end where the paste is thicker.

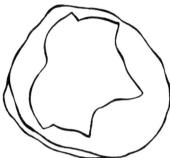

2 Take a suitable length of cotton-covered wire, make a small hook at one end and then moisten and insert this into the leaf. This wire will form the stem so it will have to be attached securely. Pinch the paste at this point. If the wire feels loose do not handle the leaf too much until it is dry.

3 Vein the leaf with a suitable tool. The main vein system forms an arrow shape with the other smaller veins running from it. There are no serrations along the edges of these leaves but it will be necessary to bend and curve them to give a natural appearance. Place leaves on suitably shaped foil while drying.

There are many other flowers belonging to this season which can also be used in cake decorating. Explore other possibilities by including some of your favourites or by presenting different combinations of flowers from those given in this selection.

Although this candle-shaped cake has been decorated with grapes and grape leaves, other fruits and leaves may be substituted to meet particular needs. A tall, sharp wooden spike is attached to the board and runs through the middle of the cake to keep it stable. (Instructions: Colours and Colouring Techniques, p. 11; Cylindrical Cakes, p. 15; Grapes, p. 55; Grape Leaves, p. 63.)

ABOVE: *It is always wonderful to receive a beautifully wrapped gift. Here is a delightful cake gift adorned with ribbon, grevillea and bright, sunny goodenias – a multi-purpose cake suitable for young and old. The sugar gift card is decorated with fern. (Instructions: Colours and Colouring Techniques, p. 11; Gift Cards, p. 68; Goodenia, p. 72; Grevillea, p. 73; Presenting Flowers, p. 82.)*

OPPOSITE: *This two-tiered, circular wedding cake captures the season's colours with its white camellias, golden nerines and lovely dark green leaves. The frills and flounces have been used to highlight the flora and also reflect the frills and flounces of many bridal gowns. (Instructions: Colours and Colouring Techniques, p. 11; Frills, p. 26; Camellia, p. 58; Nerine, p. 62; Foliage, p. 63; Ribbons, p. 82.)*

WINTER

Winter is the season of rest and renewal when nature appears to slumber. It is a time of few flowers but many beautiful, lacy branches. Winter flora is either small and bright or large and fragile and the muted tones of blue and grey are particularly attractive. Decorations for winter reflect the flora of the season and many Australian natives have been included since they offer a bright, cheery tone. Flowering periods vary, of course, with location and climate.

A vase cake decorated with Cooktown orchids, happy wanderer and correa, contrasting with winter branches, and a gift cake presented with bright goodenia and grevillea flowers, are suitable for birthdays and anniversaries or just for saying thanks. Cakes for special occasions, such as weddings or engagements, can be decorated with ribbon roses or sugar rhododendrons and wattle. A coming of age cake, in the form of a rectangle with a Florentine design, is also included. Cakes with sailing ships in floodwork can be used for many celebrations including *bon voyage* parties.

Extension Work

This is also known as bridge or curtain work. It is very pretty but also very fragile and time consum-

This two-tiered winter wedding cake, baked in corner-cut rectangular tins, displays mauve rhododendrons, wattle and silver-green foliage. The leaves, in pairs along the stems, are almost heart-shaped. The sprays have been arranged in sheaf bouquets so that the stems are visible. Extension work is a feature, and the embroidery design reproduces a small stem of wattle. (Instructions: Colours and Colouring Techniques, p.11; Embroidery, p.43; Extension Work, p.65; Place Cards, p.68; Rhododendron, p.76; Wattle, p.77; Presenting Flowers, p.82; Ribbons, p.82.)

ing. It is the line work seen on the base of many show cakes and consists of a series of fine parallel lines piped onto a bridge. They are spaced no further apart than the width of one strand. The lower bridge is built up by piping layers of icing one upon the other until they stand out from the cake. The lines are then piped from the cake surface to the base of this bridge. Since the work is so fragile and time consuming it may be best to reserve it for show entries.

If the cake is to have embroidery as well as extension work it is best to do this first to avoid damage.

Method

1   Cut a strip of greaseproof paper the same size

as the circumference. Fold the paper according to the number of scallops required. Draw the scallop pattern from fold to fold. Make an additional fold in the paper which is no higher than one-third the height of the cake. This line will indicate the height of the extension. Use pinpricks to mark the scallop pattern through the folds of the paper. Transfer the line and scallop pattern onto the cake.

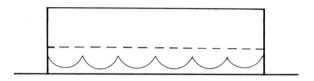

2 Pipe a very fine line of beading at the base of the cake between the cake and the board. Use a soft-peak royal icing and a No. 1 tube.

3 Use a soft-peak icing and an icing bag fitted with a No. 1–3 writing tube. Any of these tubes will be suitable; the size will be a matter of choice. Following the pinpricks, pipe scallops around the cake being sure none touch the board, or the beading. Once these are dry, return and pipe a second layer over the first and continue in this way until 5–8 layers have been piped. Remember that these scallops should be as smooth as possible with no spaces between each layer.

4 Using a soft-peak royal icing and an icing bag fitted with a No. 00 or 000 tube, pipe a series of fine lines. These should commence at the line above the scallops and finish on the bridge. It is a good idea to pipe a line at each end of the scallop and also one in the centre, before filling in the remaining area. This will help keep the lines straight during piping.

Pipe these lines in the same way as other lines (see Lines, p. 44). That is, commence with a dot and continue piping while holding the thread suspended from the cake. Drop this down onto the bridge when it is long enough and then finish it off with a quick down and under movement. It will be helpful if the cake top is slanted towards the body

because this will allow the strands to fall away from the cake and onto the bridge. Continue with this work until the whole area has been filled with these lines.

5 Once the extension has been completed, it can be finished off. You could use a row of dots or beading at the top and base where the lines commence and finish. Small scallops can be piped at the base and lace can be attached above the commencement line. You can also hailspot each line or pipe a second layer of lines in a criss-cross pattern.

Sugar Ornaments

Although many items come under this heading, this chapter will deal with plaques as well as some less frequently presented ornaments.

Sugar Plaques

These can be made from the soft icing used for covering cakes, Gum Paste (see recipe, p. 97), or combinations of the two. In winter, or in very humid conditions, it is recommended they be made from Gum Paste. Tragacanth gum can also be added to the sugar to aid drying.

Method

1 Work up some paste so that it becomes firm and pliable. It should feel much firmer than the paste used for flower making but it must still be pliable enough to be rolled without breaking and crazing.

2 Roll out the paste so that it is 2–3 mm thick and large enough to make up the plaque. The surface of the paste should be smooth and craze-free so repeat the rolling until this has been achieved. A variety of cutters can be used for making plaques or they can be cut freehand with an art knife. Cut out a suitably shaped piece of paste and then smooth down the outer edges. Once completed, place it on a piece of paper to allow for easy turning during the drying process. Allow two to three days for drying and turn the plaque over twice daily. This will reduce distortion so that the finished item will be smooth and flat.

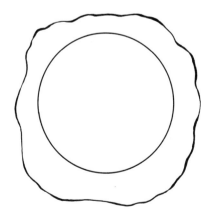

Patterns can be indented on the outer edge of these plaques. To avoid cracking, this should be done while the paste is still moist. Patterns can be made from household items such as the top of fancy spoons.

Plaques can be used for floodwork, flower arrangements or greetings. These decorations are done prior to placing the plaque on the cake. They can be stored for many months, either decorated or plain. They are ideal for occasions when the decoration on a cake is to be removed and kept.

Serviette Rings

These can be tailor-made for any occasion. They can be decorated with the same ornaments as those used on the cake or they can be individual gifts.

Method

1 Work up some paste in the same way as you did for the Sugar Plaques. Roll out the paste in long strips about 2–5 cm wide. Take an empty cardboard roll out of a roll of greaseproof paper or something similar and cover it with a layer of waxed paper. Roll the strips of paste onto the roll and attach the joins securely. Moisten one end and overlap the other. Press gently. Set these aside to dry for two to three days.

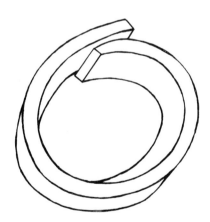

2 If fancy holders are required, the joins can be treated a little differently. Roll the paste out into slightly longer strips. Join the paste where the ends meet by moistening with a little water. Twist and curve the ends so they look like two arum lilies. Use more pieces of paste to make up another two flowers and insert these beside the others. Roll out a thin sausage and insert a piece into each of the flower centres. The result will give the effect of a stigma at the centre of each flower. Set the rings aside to dry before colouring the flower centres.

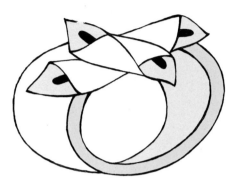

The plain rings can be decorated with moulded sugar flowers or leaves. Names may also be used as an ornament on these rings.

Place Cards

For those special occasions, individual sugar place cards add that finishing touch.

Method

1 Make up a quantity of paste in the same way as you did for the Sugar Plaques. Roll this out and cut the required number of cards. They can be square or rectangular. Small sugar stands can be made or you can use a large amount of paste and fold it. Experiment a little until your ideal place card has been produced. As a guide for names indent a line into the card by pressing a small skewer in the appropriate space.

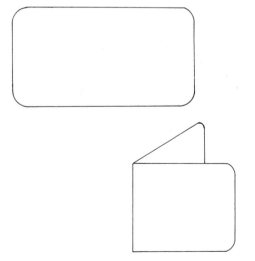

2 Allow these cards to dry thoroughly and then pipe or paint names on them. The corners can be painted with a little gold or silver, or very small moulded flowers can be attached with a little royal icing.

Gift Cards

Method

1 Gift cards can be made in the same way as folded place cards. Put them on a small piece of cardboard or perspex to ensure the fold is not lost during the drying process. Set these aside for two to three days for drying.

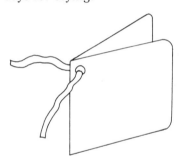

2 Once the cards are dry, they can be decorated with small moulded flowers or floodwork. Names can also be piped or painted on the inside.

Bombonnière

These small gifts filled with sugared almonds are now common gifts for guests at weddings, engagements and christenings. They can be very elaborate or quite plain. For a simple version use small, handkerchief-sized pieces of tulle to hold some sugared almonds which are then assembled with a small spray of moulded flowers or leaves. More elaborate gifts can be made up from sugar ornaments which are then filled or decorated with the tulle and almonds.

Plates and Cases

Method

Collect some small ornaments. Small butter dishes, tiny bowls or even a shallow patty tin are suitable. Make up some paste in the same way as you did for Sugar Plaques (see p. 67). Dust the ornament you have chosen with a little cornflour. Roll out the paste and then lay this over the dusted item. Press the paste all over so that any embossed pattern is transferred. Trim off any excess paste and then smooth the edges. If the paste has been embossed on the under surface, turn it over and press into shape once again. Allow the paste to set while still on the dish to ensure the shape is retained. Remove from the dish, and then set aside to dry for two to three days. Paint or decorate the dish and then add the tulle and almonds.

Chocolate moulds can be used for making plates and cases — small or medium heart shapes are particularly good.

Moulded Flowers

Cooktown Orchid

(see colour plate opposite p. 72)

Many orchid varieties can be successfully made in sugar. Because of its size, the Cooktown Orchid is particularly useful as a sugar decoration, while the shape and colour also make it very versatile.

Flower

Method

1 Take a 25 cm piece of medium cotton-covered wire and make a small hook at one end. Take a ball of paste about 1 cm in diameter and mould it between the fingers to form a short, fat bullet shape. Moisten the hooked end of the wire and then insert this into one end of the paste.

2 Next shape the paste into a curved crescent about 1–1.5 cm long and 6 mm in width. This tongue should be as flat as possible at the wire end, because the entire flower is built on the back of this section. The wire join should be as secure and smooth as possible.

3 Take a piece of paste and roll it out thinly. Then cut out a throat. Use a template or make a cutter using the drawing below.

4 Press the throat against a plastic petal to indent fine, vein-like lines in the surface. Pinch the centre base of the throat to give it a slight point. Moisten the back of the tongue and the centre back of the throat. Lay the tongue on the throat and then draw the two sides up so that they join at the centre of the top of the tongue. This join should sit snugly on the top and have a 2–3 mm overlap. This overlap looks like a very small seam. Drape the flower over a glass while the next section is made.

5 Take a piece of foil and make a slightly pointed cone in the centre, leaving the outer area flat. The point at the base will support the base of the flower and the top flat section will support the outer edges of the flower.

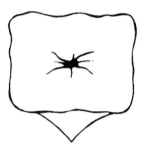

6 Take a ball of paste about 1.5 cm in diameter and form it into a long, teardrop shape which has a flat top. Pinch the edges to flatten them. Once it is large enough, roll it out with a small rolling pin. The edges should be as fine as possible but the point should be retained in the centre. The final result will be a large, wide witch's hat. Use the drawing below to cut out a three-petal shape but be sure to retain the centre peak.

7 Press the cut-out over a plastic petal to create a light veined effect. Then use a blunt tool to mark a long, centre vein in each petal. Use a suitable tool to hollow out the centre a little. Pinch the tips and

then place the piece in the centre of the foil cup being sure to curve the petals over the foil.

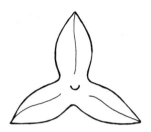

8 Roll out another piece of paste, then cut out two petals in the shape shown below. Press these against a plastic petal to indent the veins and then use the blunt end of a suitable tool to indent a long central vein in each of the petals. Moisten the lower base of each of the petals, then lay them on the triple pointed cone at ten o'clock and two o'clock. Press gently and allow some overlap so they are secure and firm.

9 Moisten the back of the throat and also the centre of the cone. Use a fine skewer to press a hole in the cone and foil. Place the throat about 5 mm from the base and to the front of the cone.

10 Take the wire end of the throat and tongue section and thread this into the hole making sure it passes through the foil. Pull the wire down through the flower, ensuring that the throat and tongue section is placed between the centre of the two lower petals. If this section needs to be moved, do so by twisting the wire to the required angle. Bend the foil if necessary to give best support. Press the foil so that the centre of the flower becomes well attached. Problems can be caused by having a pointed base at the wire end of the centre section. This can be cut away with a pair of fine scissors. Set completed flowers aside to dry thoroughly before colouring. A flat tray with a bed of cotton wool will offer the best support for this drying process. Note that the completed flower has the stem located to the front, about 5–8 mm from the cone point.

No leaves or buds will be made for this flower because they both look very heavy.

Correea alba

(see colour plate opposite p. 72)

The flower of this native shrub is a beautiful, four-petal white star, unlike most of the other correas which have a tubular flower. The flower of *Correa alba* is quite shallow in the base and will often have a slight pink tinge when still a bud.

Flower

Method

1   Take a ball of paste about 8 mm in diameter and rotate this between the fingers to shape it into a 1 cm long teardrop. Make a small hook at one end of a 12–15 cm length of fine or medium cotton-covered wire. Moisten this with water.

2   Using either a suitable tool or the handle of a paint brush, hollow out the cone. Use a forwards and backwards movement while rotating the piece of paste between the fingers and the tool. The cone should be about 13 mm in diameter. Cut it into four equal-sized sections. These will be about 8 mm deep.

3   Trim each petal by cutting a triangular piece off each corner. The petals should be rounded at the sides with a wide point at the tip. As each petal is trimmed, press the sides in and pinch the tip. This will have the effect of giving the petals a concave appearance with a pinched point at the tip. Place four stamens into the centre of the flower. These should curve out and be placed between each petal. The stamens should be about 1 cm in length.

Buds

Method

These buds are rather fat and bulbous. Take a ball of paste about 7 mm in diameter. Insert the hooked end of a 12–15 cm length of fine or medium cotton-covered wire into the paste. Pinch the base to secure the wire, then press the bud between the fingers to give it a fat, rounded appearance. Make several of these in graded sizes.

Leaf

Method

1   The leaves of this flower are small to medium-sized, and oval in shape. Take a ball of paste about 7 mm in diameter. Make a small hook at one end of a 12–15 cm piece of fine or medium cotton-covered wire. Press the moistened hook end of the wire into the paste and then flatten it between the fingers.

2   Trim the paste to make an oval-shaped leaf about 1.5 cm in length. Indent a central vein with the back of a knife blade. Twist or bend the leaf to give it a more natural appearance. Make several of these and set them aside to dry.

Leaves can be made in graded sizes, then attached along stems, representing small branches. The flowers appear close to the apex of the stems.

Dry Branches

(see colour plate opposite)

The following instructions are provided so that decorations other than just flowers and leaves can be included in arrangements. Dry stems and small pieces of driftwood all add to the beauty of an arrangement. Although these are not usually included in sugar arrangements, it is hoped they will be used more often when it is discovered how easy they are to make.

Before commencing, decide which branches you want to use and how long they will be. A wire frame can then be made for the desired shape. It may be useful to draw the stems on paper or perhaps use real samples for this work so that a guide is available.

Method

1 Draw several illustrations of the required branches or collect some suitable samples. Take several lengths of heavy and medium cotton-covered wire and twist several of these together so that they have more strength. The main branch will need to be much thicker than the others, so work according to the thickness of your branches.

2 Assemble the wires so that they begin to resemble the drawing or a sample. Depending on the size of the branches, these wires can now be covered with or encased in paste or royal icing. The larger pieces should be covered with royal icing while the smaller ones can be done in paste. It is possible to use a combination of the two icings, so it will be a matter of experimenting a little to achieve the best results. Both icings can be coloured before application so they only need to be touched up once the piece is complete. Finally, several layers can be used to help achieve a realistic thickness where necessary. Do not forget to bend and curve the wire into the desired shape well before the icing is dry, otherwise it will crack and break.

The best way to apply the paste is to roll a piece out to a small rectangle and then wrap it around the wires. Press and squeeze so that the paste adheres well. Repeat this until all the areas are covered. Royal icing should be as thick as possible and applied with the aid of a spatula. Use the hands to squeeze and smooth the icing over the wire surfaces.

Once the wires have been completed, they should be placed upright in a suitable container or vase. These items will dry more quickly if the air can circulate freely around them.

Note that Corkscrew Willow branches make very interesting decorations, since they are not too thick but have many twists and turns to give them character.

Goodenia

(see right colour plate between pp. 64–65)

The Goodenia flowers are usually brilliant yellow, but some varieties are a deep blue. As there are many varieties of Goodenia and they flower at different times, the flowering season extends almost for the entire year. The flowers have three petals on the lower half of the flower and two above. They all have crinkled edges and appear to have small, v-like sections missing from the tips.

A vase-shaped cake decorated with a variety of winter blooms offers unlimited possibilities. Dry looking corkscrew willow branches made from sugar make an ideal backdrop for the Cooktown orchids. The happy wanderer is used for its draping effect and the star-like correa completes the natural looking arrangement. A tall, sharp wooden spike is attached to the board and runs through the middle of the cake to keep it stable. (Instructions: Colours and Colouring Techniques, p. 11; Cylindrical Cakes, p. 15; Cooktown Orchid, p. 69; Correa alba, p. 71; Dry Branches, p. 72; Happy Wanderer, p. 75; Presenting Flowers, p. 82.)

ABOVE: A vision of winter is depicted on this circular cake. The unusual and dramatic scene can be used for many occasions. (Instructions: Floodwork, p. 54; Floodwork Colouring, p. 55.)

OPPOSITE: In this classical cake design the traditional key has been replaced with a rectangle. A second overlay or partial covering has been placed on the cake and allowed to dry. Small shaped pieces have been cut out of the same icing, moistened with a little egg white and then attached below the line of the second covering. The embroidery ensures these pieces look like eyelet or cutout work. A small overlay 21 has been placed on the cake and a Florentine design painted around the numerals. (Instructions: Colours and Colouring Techniques, p. 11; Overlay Covering, p. 21; Eyelet Work, p. 48; Floodwork, p. 54.)

Flower

Method

1 Take a ball of paste about 8 mm in diameter and roll it between the fingers to form a teardrop. Use the handle of a paint brush or some other suitable tool to hollow out the paste to a fine, thin cone. Divide the cone into five petals; cut the paste so that the top consists of one-third and the base is two-thirds. Trim away a small wedge from both sides of each cut, then divide the top part into two equal petals and the bottom part into three equal-sized petals.

2 Trim away a small v-shape from the centre tip of each petal. Lay the flower on a piece of rubber and gently frill or ball the outer edges of the petals. These edges should not be too frilly. They are meant to be crinkled and accentuate the central line which is formed by this process. Slightly overlap the top petals and curve them back a little. The three base petals should curve down and be spaced out.

3 Take a 15 cm piece of fine or medium cotton-covered wire and make a small hook at one end. Moisten this and insert it into the flower. Work from the inside and pull it through the flower so that it comes out at the back. Then pinch the base to secure it firmly.

A tall, chocolate-topped croquembouche makes a wonderful wedding cake, beautifully adorned with ribbon roses. (Instructions: Ribbon Roses, p. 77; Ribbons, p. 82; Recipes, p. 97.)

Calyx

Method

Cut five small sections into the base of the flower but do not cut the paste off completely. The idea is to have five, fine-pointed sections still attached to the base of the flower. Press and pinch the tips and turn them back a little.

Buds

Method

Take a ball of paste about 7 mm in diameter and roll it between the fingers to make a blunt bullet shape. Insert the moistened, hooked end of a 15 cm piece of fine or medium cotton-covered wire. Pinch and squeeze the base to attach it securely. Cut five sections at the base of the bud in the same way as for the calyx on the flower.

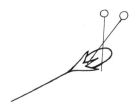

Since the leaves of this plant can be rather straggly it is best to use the leaves from another plant when arranging these flowers.

Grevillea

(see right colour plate between pp. 64–65)

There are many varieties of this shrub. Flowers come in very small, almost insignificant sizes and shapes. The method described is versatile and can be adapted according to your needs. Always endeavour to have a real sample or photograph nearby to ensure accuracy.

Grevillea are made up of a number of sections of small flowers which are assembled when dry. Flowers can be represented as open or unfurling, which means that the stamens are either fully open or tightly curled up into the flower.

No leaf instructions are given for grevillea due to the many varieties.

Flower

There are two methods that can be used here: one for piped flowers and one for moulded flowers.

Method A

1 This method is a piped version made from royal icing. Make up a firm royal icing either in white or a suitable colour. Place some icing into a piping bag which has no tube in it. Cut a hole in the tip of the bag; it should be large enough to allow for comfortable piping. Experiment a little, starting with 2 mm in diameter, to see if it is suitable for the size of your flower.

2 Pipe a large, fat comma. Commence by placing a sheet of waxed paper onto a board. Pipe a large, round dot and then while still pressing the icing, move the tip of the bag in a circular motion and form a large, widely spaced comma. Pipe a series of these on the paper and allow them to dry.

3 Once these are dry, gently lift them off the paper and turn them over so that the flat side is facing up. Take a long stamen and bend it by pressing it between the fingers. Secure a piece of wire to the cotton end and then lay it on the flat, dry, half flower. The stamen should curve in the same direction as the comma and the wire join should be in the centre of the flower. The waxed part should protrude about 1.5 cm further from the end of the flower. Pipe another comma over the dry one. Set aside to dry completely before colouring.

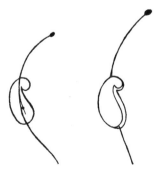

Method B

1 Take a stamen and curve the full length of the cotton by running it between the fingers. Be sure to scrape the stamen against a fingernail as you pull it between the fingers; this will ensure that it stretches and curves. Take a ball of paste 5 mm in diameter and insert the stamen into it so that about 1 cm of stamen is showing at the top. Press and flatten the paste until a flat, bullet shape has been formed. It will be about 13 mm in length and 5–6 mm in width, with the stamen wedged in its centre. If a wire is to be used as the stem, cut off the stamen end at the base of the paste. Take a piece of fine cotton-covered wire about 12–15 cm in length. Form a small hook at one end, moisten this with water and insert it into the base of the flower, pinching and squeezing the paste to attach it securely.

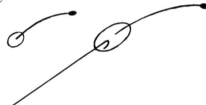

2 Press the paste at the base of the flower to form a flat, pointed end. Push the back of a scissor blade into the side of the paste about two-thirds of the way along the length. This makes a strong indentation in the paste, giving it the appearance of a comma.

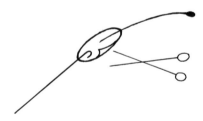

3 Gently cut into the top third of the paste. The incision should commence at the base of the indentation which has just been formed and it should end at the edge of the stamen cotton at the tip of the flower. The incision is at the side of the flower extending to the middle of the width. Make several of these flowers and then set them aside to dry thoroughly before colouring.

4 If some of the flowers are to be unfurling, bend the stamen in half and then insert into the paste.

5 Assembly of these flowers will depend on the variety of plant which is being made. Some flowers are in small, almost circular clusters, while others are formed in long, pendulous clusters which look a little like bunches of grapes. If the rounded clusters are to be formed, assemble a number of the completed flowers and then wrap a piece of cotton-covered wire around them, being sure to allow enough length for the stem. Press a finger into the centre of the bunch so that the stamens bend outwards giving a realistic appearance.

6 For flowers in a pendulous bunch, commence by assembling the smallest ones at the tip. Arrange the flowers along the top part of a long piece of wire. These can be secured by using florist's tape.

Happy Wanderer*

(see colour plate opposite p. 72)

This native plant is a twining vine with masses of purple, mauve or pink-white flowers. The small, pea flowers grow in clusters with all varieties having a slight green tinge at the tip of the central petal.

*Hardenbergia species.

Flower

Method

1 Take a very small ball of paste about 3 mm in diameter. Depending on circumstances, the wire can be short or long. If flowers are to drape down the sides of a cake, allow 20 cm. Otherwise 12–15 cm lengths will be adequate. Make a small hook at one end of fine or medium cotton-covered wire. Moisten this and then insert it into the paste. Squeeze and press the paste between the fingers to form a small 5 mm pastie shape. Use an art knife or similar to press down the length of this paste so that it appears to be two very small, attached petals.

2 Take another small ball of paste about 4 mm in diameter. Flatten this between the fingers to form a small, round petal. Cut it to look like a rounded heart. It should be pointed at the base and have a small v removed at the top to give it the heart shape. Paint a line of water down the lower half of the petal. Lay the now divided pastie along the length of this line so that the point of the heart petal is at the base line of the wire. Curve the heart petal out and under, away from the centre of the flower.

Buds

Method

Take a very small ball of paste about 3 mm in diameter. Make a small hook at one end of a fine or medium cotton-covered wire. Moisten this and then insert it into the paste. Squeeze and press between the fingers to form a 7 mm pastie shape. Press the tip of the bud between the fingers and gently bend it to give it a soft curve. Make several of these and set them aside to dry thoroughly.

Leaf

Method

Take a ball of paste which is 1.5 cm in diameter. Roll this between the fingers to form a bullet shape. Roll this out to a suitable thickness and then, using an art knife, cut out a leaf shape free-hand. The leaves of this vine vary in size but they are usually a maximum length of 6–7 cm. They are about 2 cm wide at the top descending to a rounded point at the base. The central vein is very pronounced and this can be marked in with the back of a knife blade. Insert a hooked piece of fine or medium cotton-covered wire. Make several leaves and set them aside to dry.

Rhododendron

(see colour plate opposite p. 65)

These flowers appear in clusters at the apex of thick stems. The plant can vary in height from a low shrub to a small tree. Rhododendrons have flowers in a variety of shapes and colours but they all have a basic cone shape which divides into five petals. Four of the five petals are the same size while the fifth is wider. This fifth petal has a soft, spotted pattern within the throat, similar to the spotted effect on orchids.

Flower

Method

1 Take a piece of either fine or medium cotton-covered wire which is 12–15 cm in length. Make a small hook at one end and moisten it. Take a ball of paste about 1.5–2 cm in diameter and attach this to the wire. Pinch the paste at the base so that it is neat and secure.

2 Roll the paste between the palms to form a cone or teardrop shape which is 3–4 cm in length. Using a hollowing tool or the handle of a brush, hollow out the centre so that the outer edges are fine and smooth.

3 For the large flower, the hollowed cone will be 4 cm wide by 4 cm in depth. Make five cuts into the cone so that it is divided into four equal petals and a fifth larger one. The divisions should be about 1 cm deep. Cut the outer edges of the petals to give them a soft rounded curve.

4 Lay the cone onto a thin piece of rubber, then use either the handle of a paint brush or a cocktail stick to frill the outer edges of each petal. Place the tool on the edge of the petal, then with a forwards and backwards rolling motion, press down on the paste. The result should be a thinner, frilly outer edge. Work the petals from left to right. Be sure to brush aside the right edge of each petal before commencing the next one. This will avoid damage to the edges.

5 Take nine stamens which are a little shorter than the cone. Bend these, and then using a pair of tweezers, insert them into the base. If the flower seems too dry for these to adhere, it may be necessary to pipe a very small amount of royal icing at the base. Finally, insert another stamen which is a little longer than the cone to represent the stigma. When complete, set aside to dry thoroughly before colouring.

Buds

Method

1 Take a 12–15 cm piece of fine cotton-covered wire. Make a small hook at one end and moisten with water. Insert into the wire a ball of paste about 1 cm in diameter, being sure to squeeze and press the paste at the base to attach securely.

2 Roll the paste between the palms or fingers to form a bullet shape. The two ends should come to a gentle point while the centre should be fatter.

3 Use either the blades of a pair of scissors or some other suitable tool to make indentations along the top half of the bud. These lines represent the unfurling petals. Set aside to dry when complete.

Leaf

The leaves of this plant are quite large. However a smaller version can be useful in an arrangement.

Method

1 Take a 12–15 cm piece of fine cotton-covered wire, make a small hook at one end and moisten with water. Take a ball of paste about 2.5 cm in diameter and mould this onto the wire, being sure to squeeze and press the paste at the base so that it is neat and securely attached.

2 Flatten the paste either by pressing it between the fingers or by rolling it out with a small rolling pin. The leaf will need to be about 5–6 cm in length.

3 Use either an art knife or a pair of scissors to cut out a leaf shape which is gently pointed at the tip. The widest part of the leaf will be 1–1.5 cm across. Mark a central vein with the blade of a pair of scissors or with another suitable tool. Set over a handle or suitably curved piece of foil to give the leaf a more natural shape. Allow to dry thoroughly before colouring.

Wattle

(see colour plate opposite p. 65)

On dull winter days, the brilliant golds of wattle or mimosa are a beautiful sight. The flowers range in colour from very pale cream to striking yellow and gold. The shape of the flowers also varies with some appearing in small tight balls while others are long and cylindrical. It should be noted that the flower of this plant is made up entirely of a mass of stamens, but the sugar version is moulded from balls of paste which are then covered in sugar crystals.

Flower

Method

1 This flower can be made in any size so adjust the size of the paste accordingly. Take a length of fine or medium cotton-covered wire and several short lengths of very fine wire. Attach the small wires at right angles to the long piece, forming several right angle junctions along the length of wire.

2 Take a small ball of paste about 3–5 mm in diameter and attach it to one of the ends of the cross wires. Continue until all the ends have a ball

attached to them. Make several of these and set aside to dry thoroughly.

3 Once the stems are complete they can be coloured. Colour the stems by using methylated spirits to dilute the colours. Take each stem and roll it in a bed of sugar crystals so that the moisture attracts a complete covering. Set these aside to dry on paper towelling so that any excess moisture may be absorbed. The wattle will look more realistic if the short wires are drawn closer together.

Ribbon Roses

(see colour plate opposite p. 73)

There are many occasions when it is necessary to decorate a cake with flowers not made from sugar. Non-traditional cakes often look best adorned with ribbon flowers. On occasions when a cake has to be transported long distances, these less fragile flowers may be more suitable.

Flower

Method

1 Use several metres of suitable ribbon for making these flowers. Satin or paper ribbon in widths of 2–8 cm are best for this work. Note that the thinner the ribbon, the smaller the finished flower.

2 Take the ribbon in the left hand and hold it so that the shiny side faces up and the length is drawn from the left. Using the left hand twist the ribbon down and back away from the body, while holding the other end of the ribbon with the right hand. Turn the right hand forward towards the body. A small, shiny triangular section will be formed at the end of the ribbon.

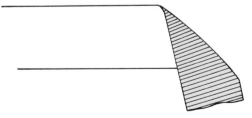

3 Use the right hand to fold about half of this triangle. The movement for this work is a right to left turning motion. The triangle needs to be folded or curved into a small, tight curve or roll, which looks like a tight cone curving in and down. At this point, the flower centre can be stitched to hold it firmly but when you have gained some experience, this may not be necessary.

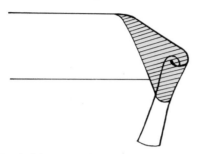

4 Use the left hand to fold another triangular section along some of the ribbon length next to the area being worked. Do this by turning the left hand back and down but do not make the triangle too long.

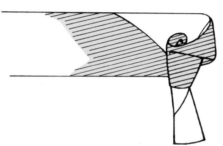

5 Repeat the folding and curving motion so that half of this triangle is rolled and curved also. The flower is made up by repeating the rolling and turning process. As the flower is forming, it is best to allow the curves to fall down and in, giving some depth to the appearance. Repeat the process until the flower is as large as required.

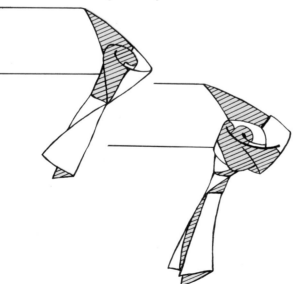

6 Once a large enough flower has been formed, take the ribbon end from the left and pinch it into the base of the flower. Hold it in place and then slip a hooked piece of wire on the inside of this end so that the wire is held between the ribbon and the thumb. Twist and bend the wire to wrap it around the base several times. Pull the end down to form a stem and then trim off the remainder of the ribbon. Use some florist's tape to bind the base of the flower ensuring the wires are hidden, then cover the wire stem. Several of these roses are required for an arrangement.

Note that if these flowers are wound too tightly they will be heavy and difficult to assemble. It is also necessary to ensure the folding remains in a triangular shape so the flower has a uniform shiny and dull appearance giving the illusion of a real rose.

Buds

Method

The buds are formed by repeating steps 1–3 of the flower. That is, the first triangle is formed and then rolled for half the length. The ribbon is then trimmed, a hooked piece of wire is placed against the folded section and then the left and right sections are folded inwards until they join. Be sure to overlap one section just a little. Wrap florist's tape around the base and down the wire stem in the same way as for the flower. Make several of these for an arrangement.

Winter provides opportunities to develop cakes of classical beauty. It is an appropriate time to develop designs with wonderful contrasts since nature displays her own contrasts of colour and form in this season.

SPRING

Spring is the season of new life: a time of beginnings and the promise of things to come. It is the time when the greatest number of plants display a profusion of colour. It is also a season of many celebrations.

The flowers in this section reflect the usual flora of the season, but, as with the other seasons, there may be some variations in flowering times depending on location. Flowering periods may also vary according to climate.

New life is reflected in the cakes designed for this season. A new moon provides the theme for a baby's christening cake. Birds preparing a home of periwinkles make a wonderful decoration for a home warming, a wedding, a birthday or an engagement cake. Spring is a popular time for weddings and happily it provides an endless selection of suitable flora such as clematis, wisteria and lilacs for decorations. The shapes of the spring wedding cakes are specially designed to provide the best presentation for spring flowers. This season also provides further opportunities for experimenting with differently shaped cakes, such as the spring hat with broom and coastal rosemary and the bridal pillow with a spray of bridal veil broom.

Writing

Many decorators like to be able to pipe a greeting on a cake or plaque. The quality of piped writing can improve considerably with just a little knowledge and plenty of practice. The main point to remember is that writing consists of lines and curves no matter what style is being used.

To begin with, simply practise short and long lines. Then practise horizontal and vertical lines. Finally, try some curved letters or a row of Cs and then join them together.

Once you have gained confidence, obtain the type of lettering book used by sign writers. Choose different writing styles and try out several greetings using pen and paper. Ensure that they are a suitable size for cakes. Practise them with a pen for a while until the result is perfect. Once you have done this, you can begin to pipe the messages on a practice sheet.

Always use free-flowing, soft-peak icing (see p. 99) for this work to avoid blocking the tube. This work can be practised freehand. Alternatively, if extra practice is required, place a copy of the message under a sheet of waxed paper. Use the left hand to support the right hand while working. Stop after every few letters so that your piping will look even. Once you are confident you can begin to pipe the message on the cake itself.

If you need a guide the cake can be marked with two very faint lines at the top and bottom of the letters. These lines can also be marked to indicate the width of each letter. If professional cakes are checked thoroughly, it is often possible to detect these guide lines.

It is worth remembering that a beautiful, individually made cake often does not require a greeting. If the cake is made especially for the occasion it will usually express all that you would wish to say. Do not spoil a cake by making a message too long.

Sugar Birds

Birds reproduced in sugar make ideal cake ornaments. A variety of birds are used as symbols of purity, love and peace, making sugar replicas appropriate for cakes or bombonnière. Many species of birds are used as a symbol of fidelity for occasions such as weddings and engagements. Birds can also be used to symbolise fertility, farewells and welcomes. Rosellas or kookaburras can be used for Australian themes. The following instructions can be adapted to suit many other types of birds.

Before commencing work on these pieces, collect some photographs or drawings of the selected birds. Be sure these include as many angles as possible including at least one side view. This will assist you to gain a clear picture of a bird's normal pose and shape. Rosellas, for example, have a long, oval shape with a nice, long tail which enhances that shape. The beak is turned down so the face looks fairly flat. Blue wrens and robins have small, slender bodies with short, close wings and small, pointed beaks. Check for these and other distinguishing features before commencing work.

Blue Wren

(see colour plate opposite)

Method

1 Use gum paste, soft icing or a combination of the two for making these birds. Work up a suitable quantity of paste to make the required number of birds. Take a ball of the paste and pull it into an appropriate shape. The wren has a pear-like shape which slants forward. Insert small pieces of wooden skewer into this paste to support the

This circular cake was baked with a small bowl placed in the mixture so that a round depression was formed on one side. The top surface has been cut to form a slant to accentuate the nest. Periwinkle flowers and foliage have been used to line the nest and a pair of blue wrens complete the scene. The embroidery work imitates a variety of satin stitch. This is a cake for weddings and anniversaries when something a little different is required. (Instructions: Colours and Colouring Techniques, p. 11; Cake Shapes, p. 15; Satin Stitch, p. 50; Stem Stitch; p. 51; Blue Wren, p. 80; Presenting Flowers, p. 82; Periwinkle, p. 91; Cake Designs, p. 104.)

shape, and make sure they cross each other within the icing. The ends should not protrude.

method used, this tail is usually at an 80 degree angle to the body.

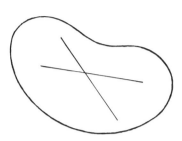

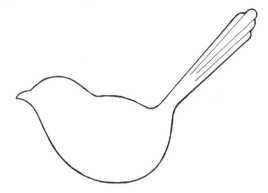

2 Smooth the paste all over. Remove all creases or at least ensure they are on the underside of the bird.

3 Take the bird's body in your hands and encircle the top, head part with your thumb and index finger. Squeeze a little to achieve the appearance of a neck and head. This will use up approximately the top third of the paste. Pull and pinch some paste at the centre front of the head to represent the beak but do not make this too large.

5 Use a small pair of scissors to cut a pair of wings from the main body of the paste. The wren's wings are small and light so it will not be necessary to cut out large pieces of paste. Cut a small triangular section on the left and right of the body making sure the wings created remain attached. Press and smooth these and trim where necessary. Pull them out a little from the body. Insert wires at the base of the body to form the legs. Use a tool or skewer to indent any special markings on the bird's body or head. Then set the bird aside to dry.

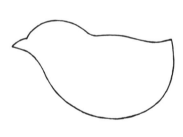

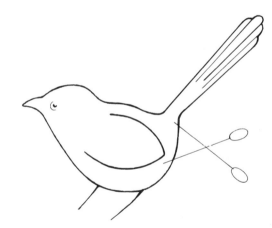

4 The tail feathers on the wren are very fine and tall. The tail can be made from an elongated piece of paste or from separate pieces. Regardless of the

6 Once the bird has dried, other details can be included. Features such as feathers and eyes can be piped in royal icing. The legs should be covered with icing using either royal or soft icing. Press the icing into, and against, the wires. Smooth it to look like slender legs. Bend the wires to form three-clawed feet and cover these as well. Once completed, the bird should be allowed to dry again and then coloured according to need. Wrens are pale brown when juvenile. The female remains this colour but the male changes as it develops. The tail of a non-breeding adult is blue. However, once the bird is mature, the tail, breast, head and part of the back become blue.

A pillow cake for a very young bride represents the page boy's ring pillow. It is made by building up the icing on the top of a square cake. The sheaf bouquet is made from the broom flowers appropriately known as bridal veil. (Instructions: Colours and Colouring Techniques, p. 11; Cake Shapes, p. 15; Frills, p. 26; Presenting Flowers, p. 82; Bridal Veil Broom, p. 86.)

Presenting Flowers

Just as real flowers are used as a guide for making sugar flowers so, too, observation of nature can assist with presentation. It is also very helpful to check the pages of a few good floral arrangement books to get more ideas for colour, form, and composition of an arrangement. Although sugar ornaments require more delicate handling because of their fragility, they can be presented as well as the real thing. The following hints will help presentation of flowers whether they are made up into free-standing sprays or set into sugar on a cake.

Presentation Hints for Sugar Flowers

□ Sugar leaves and flowers need to be wired together so they can be arranged realistically.

□ Many flowers grow in a spiral formation along the length of stems. If sugar replicas are to be presented, it is best to use an adapted version. Although it is an easy matter to reproduce a spiral effect, flowers on the rear of the stem may break and they are not visible.

□ The flowers of some of the larger varieties grow at the apex of stems. This need not create problems. Florists use wire to help hold the particular shape of individual flowers or sprays; the cake decorator can use this method as well.

□ Clusters or florets need to be presented more sparsely than in nature to avoid breakages.

□ Leaves, ferns and other greenery can be used to help provide contrast. Arrangements using these appear more natural and can also reduce the number of flowers required.

□ Ribbons can also be used within arrangements to improve contrast and reduce the number of flowers required. Fine, narrow ribbon is traditionally used on cakes but a combination of narrow and wider ribbon can be very effective. Reasonably narrow, picot-edged ribbon can also be used.

□ It is not essential to present flowers in a formal spray. Single stems of flowers and leaves can be a pretty alternative. For the less formal wedding cake, place a small bunch of flowers tied with pretty ribbon on the top of the cake.

□ Regardless of which presentation method is used, always reserve spare flowers and leaves. These can be arranged wherever required to disguise any signs of assembly or to hide wires.

Ribbons

Ribbons are used extensively in cake decorating, generally to soften or extend flower arrangements. Ribbons can be made into small clusters of loops, loops with trailing tails, or just trails. When used within posy arrangements, figure-eight bows can be very effective.

Figure-eight Bow

Wide ribbons are more suitable for this work although several bows of thin ribbon can be combined to give a soft effect.

Method

1 Take a length of ribbon in the left hand and form a loop at one end, incorporating that end and leaving the rest trailing. Pinch the loop at its join with your fingers, then make another loop opposite the first with the trailing part of the ribbon to give a figure-eight bow. Continue in this way forming pairs of loops until you have four pairs. Make sure the ribbon is placed dull side to dull side with the shiny side facing out.

2 Once the eight loops have been formed, make a ninth, much longer loop, making sure that all of the trailing end is incorporated. Use a piece of wire to bind the loops together at their centre points where you have been holding them. The wire should form a 'u' as it is placed around the ribbon. Pull the two ends of the wire down and give one or two twists under the base of the ribbon. Use a pair of scissors to cut through the ninth loop to form a short and a longer trail.

Looped Ribbon

This is best made with fine, narrow ribbon. It is ideal for use in sprays which do not require very much ribbon or placed in a spray which is to be built into a base of icing.

Method

Take some ribbon and form short loops, placing the ribbon dull side to dull side so the shiny side is facing out. Make odd numbers of loops, such as three or five, then take a piece of wire and wrap it around their base. The wire should form a 'u' as it is placed around the ribbon. Twist the wire at the base of the ribbon but do not cut its ends off until later.

Looped Ribbon with Trails

This ribbon is made up in the same way as the looped ribbon but the two ends are left in long lengths. When these loops are wired together, the two ends become trails. These can be cut on an angle as required. If upright trails are required, these ends can be turned up before the ribbon is wired.

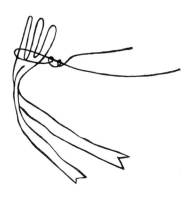

Ribbon roses can also be used as a form of decoration. These have been included in the Winter section (see p. 77).

Sprays and Bouquets

Before sugar leaves and flowers can appear realistic they need to be made up into small sprays. Flowers can be held together with wire, then the stems covered with florist's tape. To use florist's tape successfully, it should first be stretched and then wrapped around the wire stems. It is self-sticking so, with pressing, it will form smooth, firm stems. Flowers can be wired individually or in groups to form small sprays.

Sprays usually consist of small groupings of flowers while bouquets are traditionally larger, more formal arrangements. In cake decorating, bouquets usually consist of a number of small sprays assembled together. This helps to reduce breakages and also makes an arrangement more manageable. It is suggested that several small sprays be made first. The stems or wires can then be arranged within a piece of icing on the cake.

Buds and small flowers should be placed at the tip of each spray, with larger flowers at the centre. Leaves can be included on separate stems or wired onto the same stem as the flowers.

Before making sprays, colour your flowers as well as some of the wire. The part closest to the flower can be coloured green, brown, or a combination of suitable tones. This will allow a little more flexibility since the whole stem will not have to be covered with florist's tape. Fuchsias are a good example of this sort of presentation. The non-taped part of the wire would help these flowers look more pendulous producing a more realistic effect.

Several varieties of flowers and leaves may be assembled into single, main stems by wiring them together with florist's tape. Remember to place the smallest flowers at the tip of the stem and to incorporate the largest flowers at the other end. Leaves may be interspersed with flowers along the stem. A portion of the wire of each flower may be left untaped. A tighter and more compact arrangement is achieved if no wire is left showing. In either case, a small bouquet will require several main stems to be assembled together. Do not use too many large flowers, however, or the focal point of your arrangement may be lost.

Alternatively, it is possible to cover all wire stems individually with florist's tape and then assemble these into sprays. Florist's tape is very adhesive so it is possible to form an arrangement by pressing the stems together in the required shape. Just hold the spray together and press wherever they need to be joined. Several of these small sprays may be assembled together to form a small bouquet.

Posy Bouquet

This arrangement is round and can be made in graded sizes to match the size of the cake. A posy may have frills or ribbon loops as a backing.

Method

1 Make one or more Figure-eight Bows from a length of ribbon (see p. 82). The number of bows will be determined by the size of the posy and the width of the ribbon.

The flowers are arranged in order of size; the largest first and the smallest last. The flowers are distributed evenly within the loops. Hold the figure-eight bows in the left hand at their join and draw the first of the larger flowers through the centre of a ribbon loop. Since this flower will be the focal point of the spray, it will extend further than the others and thus determine the height of the posy.

2 Insert the next flower behind and slightly lower than the focal one, making sure it passes through a loop. Place the third flower in front of and lower than the focal flower so that now a central row of three flowers has been formed. Arrange the rest of the larger flowers clockwise around these three until a circle has been built. If the posy is to remain small, use buds around the three largest flowers.

Remember that all the stems pass through the ribbon loops and are held below them. Each flower should be bent forward slightly. The height of the flowers is graduated so that the posy is highest at its centre and lowest at its outermost circle. If you wish to add other, smaller flower varieties, such as gypsophila, insert single stems or stems of flower clusters between the larger flowers of the posy. Finally insert leaves where required. Trim the base wires according to need and then tape them together with florist's tape. Include any extra loops or trails if they are required. The central stem (made up of all the wire stems) can be inserted into a small mound of icing which has been placed on the top of the cake. It can also be bent and wrapped in plastic before being inserted into the cake covering or placed into the neck of a small cake vase.

When making posies for tiered cakes allow the ribbon trails to drape over the side of the cake.

Oval Posy

Method

1 Follow the instructions for Posy Bouquet, steps 1–2, until a central line of three larger flowers has been formed. Then insert another large flower at each end of this line so that it now consists of five flowers. Larger and smaller buds may be used instead of large flowers.

2 Continue to build up the posy in the way described for Posy Bouquet, step 2, being sure to retain the central circular shape. When the smaller flowers are placed, small, trailing sprays can be inserted at the two ends of the oval posy.

Trailer Bouquet

(see colour plate opposite p. 88)

Here a trailing piece is added to the Posy Bouquet.

Method

1 Make a posy using the same method described for the Posy Bouquet, but omit the front flower in the row of three largest flowers to leave a space in which to insert the trailing piece.

2 Make a trailing piece using a combination of the flowers and leaves used in the posy. This is like a small spray with small flowers and leaves at the tip and larger ones at the top. Make your wires a little longer than usual.

3 Insert this trailer in the space allowed for it in the posy. Pull the wire in with the posy wires and then assemble the trailer bouquet on the cake as required.

Crescent Bouquet

Method

1 Make up a posy in the way described for the Posy Bouquet, but omit the two outer flowers in the row of three so that two spaces are left for the two trailing pieces that will be inserted.

2 Make up two small trailing pieces with the same smaller and larger flowers used in the posy. One piece should be slightly smaller than the other.

3 Curve each of these two trailers and then insert them into the spaces left in the posy. Secure the wires into the central stem and wire according to need. When the bouquet is placed on the cake the longer trailer is closer to the cake edge and the shorter one is closer to the centre.

Sheaf Bouquet

(see colour plates opposite p. 65 and p. 81)

This bouquet requires flowers to be made with varying length stems or wires since the effect is achieved by the line of the spray.

Method

The spray can be made by arranging the flowers in order of size so that the buds are placed at the tip and the large ones are closer to the other, ribbon, end. Insert any other flowers and foliage alongside these main flowers. Tie the arrangement together by using either wire and ribbon or just ribbon. The ends of the stems will be visible. Do not place this type of arrangement at the centre of the cake top. Lay it as required either off centre or diagonally.

Arrangements such as the one on the vase cake (see colour plate opposite p. 72), which are placed on a cake in an upright position, follow the same principles for line and form as all the floral arrangements discussed in the book. The only difference is that, since they have to look pleasing at all angles, more flowers may be required to fill out the back of these arrangements.

Moulded Flowers

Broom

(see left colour plate between pp. 88–89)

These plants grow all over the world. Since there are so many varieties, flowers can be found in many colours although they are predominantly in shades of white, cream, and yellow. However, while there are variations between the differing plants they all have pea flowers. Some are long or wide while others are quite small. Most have trifoliate leaves although there are some that have very simple or needle-like leaves. It would be impossible to provide instructions on how to make all the attractive flowers belonging to this family. However, the following description will allow you to make a basic pea flower that you can adapt to match a particular broom you wish to copy.

Flower

Method

1 Take a ball of paste about 1 cm in diameter and roll it between the fingers to form an oval shape that becomes the central bud. Insert the moistened, hooked end of a 15 cm piece of fine or medium cotton-covered wire into one end of the oval. Press and flatten the paste but allow a little thickness in the centre. The two ends should be pointed with the tip turned up and the bud curved gently. The bud should measure 2 cm in length and 7 mm in width.

2 Take another piece of paste and roll it out as thinly as possible. Cut out two petals using the small or medium frangipani cutter. These petals need to be just a fraction shorter than the bud so choose your cutter accordingly. Ball the inside of the petals to give them a cupped shape. Moisten the pointed ends and then place them on either side of the bud. Press at the base and then use a dry brush to gently ease the rounded ends away from the bud.

3 Take another piece of paste and roll it out as thinly as possible. Use a briar rose cutter to cut out one petal. Gently fold the petal in half along the length and then open it out again. This should produce a fold line along the length of the petal. Frill the outer edges of the petal but avoid the area near the fold. Pinch the paste at the tip of the petal to accentuate it.

4 Moisten the base of the petal and then attach it to the flower. Be sure not to moisten a large area because the petal is attached only at the very base. Push the top part of the petal back and away from the flower and press very gently on the centre of the sides so that the backward slant is more obvious. Set the flower aside to dry thoroughly before colouring.

Calyx

The calyx of this flower is almost a rounded knob at the base of the flower.

Take a ball of paste which is 3 mm in diameter and knead it between the fingers to form a small cone. Push a long needle through the centre and press against the edges of the hole to enlarge it. Moisten the base of the flower and then insert the stem wire into the cone. Press the calyx paste so that it adheres to the flower base and forms a triangular shape.

Buds

Method

Follow the above flower instructions until the end of step 1. Make several buds, grading some of them

in order to achieve a more natural looking spray. Set aside to dry thoroughly before colouring.

Leaf

The leaves described are trifoliate since the needle-like ones are difficult to present.

Method

1 Take a piece of wire about 18 cm in length and twist onto one end another piece about 3–4 cm in length. Fine or medium cotton-covered wire can be used for this work. The smaller piece should be held against the longer one to form a cross. Twist the small wire around the longer piece so that it is securely fastened and will not roll around.

2 Take a ball of paste 5 mm in diameter and insert one end of the short wire into it. Press and flatten the paste, then use a small pair of scissors to cut out a leaf shape which has the wire encased within it. Repeat the process for the other two ends of wire. Mark out the veins by using the back of a knife blade. Make several of these clusters and then set aside to dry before colouring.

Bridal Veil Broom

(see colour plate opposite p. 81)

This is one of the loveliest and yet most inconspicuous of flowers. Each flower is so small that it can easily be overlooked. However, as a shrub this broom is magnificent with a lovely soft fragrance when in bloom. It makes an ideal sugar flower for many occasions. It can be used as an additional flower in a spray or made into a spray on its own. The flowers are white with a deep burgundy tint at the very base.

Flower

Method

1 Take a ball of paste which is 3 mm in diameter. Depending on how you are going to use the flowers, it may be advisable to use 20 cm lengths of wire. Fine or medium cotton-covered wire should be used. Make a small hook at one end, moisten it and shake off any excess water. Insert the wire into the paste.

2 Flatten the paste to form a small, slightly oval, flat centre about 7–9 mm in length. Trim off any excess or cut the piece to the required shape if necessary.

3 Take another ball of paste about 3 mm in diameter and roll this between the fingers to form a short sausage. The ends should be pointed while the centre needs to be a little fatter. Press this between the fingers to flatten. This piece will need to become 1.5 cm in length and 3 mm in width. Cut it in half along the length. Moisten along the base of the petals, where they have been cut, with a little water and then attach them to the central piece on either side of the centre pushing them out and back so that they look like two wings.

4 Take another ball of paste which is 3 mm in diameter and squeeze this between the fingers to form a small, flat, oval petal. Trim this almost to a point at each end. Gently fold the petal in half along the length and then open it out again. Moisten one end and attach it to the rear base of the flower. It will be placed over the base of the two previous petals. Be sure the indentation of the fold is to the front of the flower. Set aside to dry thoroughly.

Buds

Method

1 Take a piece of wire which is much the same size and thickness as that used for the flower. Make

a small hook at one end and moisten, being sure to shake off any excess water. Take a ball of paste which is 3 mm in diameter and attach this to the hooked end.

2 Press the paste to flatten it into a small oval shape with a slightly pointed tip. Trim any excess paste if necessary or cut the paste to the size and shape required. Be sure to pinch the base so that it is secure, and then set aside to dry.

The leaves on this plant are long, coarse needles. Since it is undesirable to reproduce these, it will be necessary to use another form of greenery with these flowers. No calyx is required.

Clematis

(see colour plate opposite p. 88)

The clematis is a deciduous, climbing vine which has natives in every country. These plants have a profusion of flowers with a beautiful fragrance. Instructions are given for *Clematis aristata* which is a delicate Australian native. *Clematis montana* will also be described since it is grown all over the world. The main feature of these flowers is their star-like appearance.

Clematis aristata

The *Clematis aristata* flowers are white although, as they grow older, they change to a soft creamy colour. The centre is very dense with a mass of green to pale gold coloured stamens which are quite long. On first impression, these flowers look like a dense cluster of fine, petal stars.

Flower

Method

1 This flower is very fragile so you need to commence with the central stamen area. Take several stamen cottons which are at least 3 cm in length. Curve these by rubbing them between the fingers. Take a 12–15 cm piece of fine or medium cotton-covered wire and wrap it around the middle of the stamens so that there is a short and long end of wire just below them. Twist the two wire ends and then moisten the twisted area. Take a small ball of paste. Insert the long end of the wire into one end and draw the paste up to the stamens. Squeeze and pinch the paste so that it attaches neatly and securely. Remove any excess paste if necessary. The completed centre should be 5–6 mm in length and about 3 mm in width.

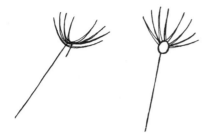

2 It is best to make the petals about 2.5 cm long and 6 mm wide. When the flowers grow wild, these petals are a third longer and a little narrower. However, since the sugar replicas can be very fragile, the above will produce a realistic alternative which should be easier to handle.

Take a small ball of paste about 6–7 mm in diameter. Roll this between the fingers to form a bullet shape. Flatten the paste between the fingers to thin it down. When it appears to be large enough, use a pair of fine scissors to trim the petals to the required shape and length or use the drawing below to make a cutter. These petals have a lovely, fine, sharp point at both ends.

3 Make four of the above petals before assembling. To assemble the flower it is necessary to moisten the bottom 3–5 mm of each petal. Attach the petals to the centre, arranging them in pairs opposite each other. This gives the flower its star appearance. The base of the flower is stronger when petals are arranged in this way since one pair helps to secure the other.

4 Bend the petals back a little but be sure the tips are slightly upturned. Press gently on the stamens to spread them out a little. It may be necessary to trim some of the stamens at this point to give the flower a realistic appearance. You will not have to trim all the stamens because this flower has a variety of stamen lengths. This is another feature which accentuates the star-like appearance.

Leaf

The leaves on this plant appear in triple clusters.

Method

1 To ensure that the leaves appear in triple clusters, it is best to make them by using the fern technique (see p. 94).

Take a 15 cm length of fine cotton-covered wire but do not make a hook at one end. Attach another piece of wire to this about 1.5 cm from the top and at right angles to the central wire. Twist the smaller wire around the centre one to attach it there, then straighten out the two ends. Once attached it should be 2.5 cm from one end to the other.

2 Take three balls of paste each about 6–7 mm in length. Roll these between the fingers, moulding them into bullet shapes. Insert the wire into the bullets. Press and flatten each piece of paste, working and completing one leaf at a time. Once the paste has been flattened it can be trimmed with a fine pair of scissors. The leaves can vary in size just as they do in nature. The smallest should be 6 mm in width by 1.5 cm in length and the largest 1 cm in width by 2.5 cm in length. Both ends of the leaves have a soft, curved point. Be sure to make each trio the same size and shape. Make several stems of leaves and set aside to dry thoroughly before colouring.

This unusual three-tiered wedding cake has been created by baking two large oval cakes. One cake is cut to form two graded and scooped half moons. Each cake has been covered with a different shade of pink icing, the smallest one having the deepest tone. The shadow stitch embroidery is in shades of pink and green. The wonderful draping cascade of native white clematis, pink Clematis montana and foliage is achieved by giving the flowers particularly long stems. (Instructions: Colours and Colouring Techniques, p. 11; Cake Shapes, p. 15; French Knots, p. 49; Shadow Stitch, p. 51; Presenting Flowers, p. 82; Ribbons, p. 82; Clematis aristata, p. 87; Clematis montana, p. 89; Cake Designs, pp. 105–107.)

ABOVE: *This hat-shaped cake is decorated with a small spray of coastal rosemary and a variety of broom flowers. The unusual shape was created by baking one 10 cm and one 15 cm round cake, and another cake in a small bowl. All three cakes were assembled together with skewers. A tall, sharp wooden spike was attached to the board and inserted through the middle of the cake to keep it stable. The brim was created by using sugar-covered cardboard. (Instructions: Colours and Colouring Techniques, p.11; Cake Shapes, p.15; Presenting Flowers, p.82; Broom, p.85; Coastal Rosemary, p.91.)*

OPPOSITE: *A baby's christening cake in the shape of a new moon has been created by baking a round cake and cutting away a portion. A collection of small sugar toys adds interest. As a finishing touch the cake has been sprinkled with stars and glitter. (Instructions: Cake Shapes, p.15; Frills, p.26; Moulded Toys, p.56.)*

Clematis montana

The flower of *Clematis montana* is much larger than that of *Clematis aristata*.

Flower

Method

1 Take a reel of white cotton and a chop-stick. Wind the cotton around the thinner end of the stick until it forms a thick ring. Slide this off the end and then insert the end of a piece of cotton-covered wire within the ring of cotton. Twist the wire so that the cotton is secured and then cut through all the loops (as you would do when making a pom-pom). Repeat the process but this time do so at the thicker end of the stick. Dip the cut ends of cotton into a thick solution of sugar and water and then set aside to dry overnight. When the two 'pom-poms' are dry place them side by side. Fan the cottons of both so that they intermingle, then twist their wires together. If required pipe a dot of royal icing in this flower centre when the flower is completed.

2 It is necessary to make four petals for this flower. These can be either made freehand or with a template or cutter. The drawing below can be used for this purpose. Take some paste and roll it out as thinly as possible and then cut out four petals. Ball each petal in the centre and at the edges to cup and frill it.

Two diamond shapes with slanted tops form a two-tiered wedding cake. The slant of the cake allows a more unusual flower presentation. The embroidery work, in a two-toned icing, displays wisteria and a double white lilac. The foliage is fern. (Instructions: Colours and Colouring Techniques, p.11; Cake Shapes, p.15; Embroidery, p.43; Presenting Flowers, p.82; Ribbons, p.82; Lilac, p.90; Wisteria, p.93; Ferns, p.94; Cake Designs, pp.108–110.)

3 This flower is assembled in the same way as *Clematis aristata*. Moisten the base of the petals and attach them to the flower centre. Arrange them in pairs facing each other. Bend and curve the petals to give the flower a natural appearance; the ends should be slightly curved with an inward slope. Make several of these flowers and set them aside to dry.

Buds

The bud of this flower appears to have a heart-like shape; it is four-faceted.

Method

1 Take a ball of paste which is 1 cm in diameter. Press it between the fingers so that a rounded base is formed and the top has a soft, slightly pointed tip.

2 Insert into the base the moistened, hooked end of a 15 cm length of fine or medium cotton-covered wire. Pinch and squeeze the base to attach it securely.

3 Press the top portion of the bud between the fingers so that it appears to have four faces.

Leaf

This clematis also has trifoliate leaves but they are much larger than those already described. It is, therefore, much easier to make these leaves individually, and then tape them together to make up clusters of three.

Method

Take some paste and roll it out so that it is thicker at one end than at the other, allowing wires to be attached. Then cut out a set of three leaves. The drawings below can be used as templates or for making up cutters. The leaves are all shaped differently so it will be necessary to arrange them in clusters according to the illustration below. Make several sets of these leaves being sure to curve and slant them so they have a natural appearance. Set these aside to dry thoroughly before colouring.

Lilac

Although lilac is considered to be rather an old-fashioned plant, its flowers are soft and delicate making them a suitable addition to many presentations. Lilac flowers are usually white, mauve or purple. Since these flowers are always in clusters it may not be obvious that they can be either singles or doubles.

Single Flower

Method

1 Take a ball of paste about 5 mm in diameter. Shape this between the fingers to a small teardrop shape which is 8 mm in length. Take a 12–15 cm length of fine or medium cotton-covered wire, make a small hook at one end and then moisten it with water. Insert the wire into the point of the teardrop, making sure you pinch it to attach it securely.

2 Use a suitable tool or the handle of a paint brush to hollow out the teardrop to a small cone. Use a forwards and backwards motion to rotate and thin down the cone, being careful to work the paste so that it thins down evenly. The diameter of the hollow cone should be about 1 cm.

3 Cut the cone into four equal parts to form four evenly shaped petals. The incisions should be about 5 mm in depth. These petals are narrow and slightly rounded so they can be squeezed and pinched into the desired shape. Alternatively, cut away small triangles from each corner and then shape them between the fingers. Because the flowers are small you will need to present several in your arrangement.

Double Flower

(see colour plate opposite p. 89)

Method

1 These flowers will have slightly more pointed petals than the singles. Take a ball of paste about 5 mm in diameter. Shape this between the fingers to a small teardrop shape which is 8 mm in length. Take a 12–15 cm length of fine or medium cotton-covered wire, make a small hook at one end and then moisten it with water. Insert the wire into the point of the cone, making sure you pinch it to attach it securely.

2 Use a suitable tool or the handle of a paint brush to hollow out the small cone in the same way you did for the Single Flower. The diameter of the hollow cone should be about 1 cm.

3 Cut the cone into four equal parts to form four evenly shaped petals. It is necessary to make the incisions about 5 mm deep. These petals are narrower than those of the single flower. They are narrow and slightly rounded at the tip. Cut away small, wedge-shaped pieces from the right side of each piece. Use a squeezing and pinching motion to then mould each petal to the desired shape. Finally, twist each petal a little to the left.

4 It is now necessary to make an identical flower to form the double. However, do not insert any wire into this one. Use the handle of a paint brush to enlarge the centre of the non-wired flower and moisten the inside with a little water. Do not use too much or the flower will disintegrate. Insert the wire from the first flower into the centre and pull down until one flower fits snugly within the other. Squeeze and pinch the base so that the paste forms a nice, smooth base. If this feels too moist, dip the fingers into cornflour before shaping. Use either a brush or the tip of a cocktail stick to bend the petals to an appropriate shape. Set aside to dry thoroughly.

Coastal Rosemary*

(see left colour plate between pp. 88–89)

This hardy shrub should be very familiar since it is often grown in parks and along roadsides. These plants flower all year round although more prolifically in spring.

Flower

Method

1 Take a ball of paste which is 8 mm in diameter. Roll the paste between the fingers to form a teardrop which is 12 mm in length. Insert into the base a 12–15 cm piece of fine or medium cotton-covered wire which has a small hook at one end moistened with water.

2 Use a suitable tool or the handle of a paint brush to hollow out the paste to form a cone as described in Single Flower (see p. 90). Divide the cone by cutting it into four equal parts to form a cross as illustrated. The depth of the petals should be 5–7 mm.

3 Trim the top and bottom petals to give the edges a rounded look. Trim the two side petals a little more severely so that they look just a little square or straight, even though their outer edges are rounded. Ball the petals at the outer tips. The top petal is bent forward into the flower while the side ones curve outward slightly. Squeeze the bottom petal a little to give it a cupped effect. Insert a cocktail stick partially into the cone to restore the original shape.

Buds

Method

Take a small ball of paste which is 4 mm in diameter. Press this between the fingers to form a short,

Westringia species.

fat bud. Take a piece of fine or medium cotton-covered wire and make a small hook at one end. Moisten this with water and shake off any excess before inserting it into the base of the bud. Squeeze and pinch the paste to form a bud shape. Make sure that the wire is attached securely.

Calyx

The buds have a very shallow, five-sepalled calyx. Once again, because the calyx is small, it is necessary to make it by cutting into the base of the bud. Using just the tip of the blades of a pair of scissors, make five small cuts in the base. These sections should still remain attached to the bud.

Periwinkle

(see colour plate opposite p. 80)

These flowers grow so vigorously that they are often considered weeds. However they make very attractive, moulded flowers. There are two varieties, one with green leaves, and the other with variegated ones. Both varieties have mauve flowers which are the same shape and tone.

Flower

Method

1 Take a piece of paste and roll it between the fingers to form a cone which is about 2 cm in length and 7 mm wide at the top of what will become the flower.

2 Hollow out the cone using any suitable tool until it is about 3–4 cm in depth and about the same in width. Remember the thinner the cone, the finer your petals will be.

3 Using a fine pair of embroidery scissors, cut the cone into five equal petals which are half as deep as the cone.

4 Open out the petals by pressing a finger down into the centre of the cone. The pressure should be applied across the centre top part of the flower. Using a cocktail stick or similar push down into the lower base of the flower. It may be necessary to squeeze the lower cone section against the stick to achieve a narrow cone appearance. This is done by holding the stick in one hand, rotating the flower in the other, and pressing against the stick.

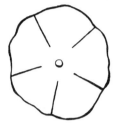

5 Press five small indentations into the base of the flower. These are placed so that they are in the centre of the base of each petal. This can be done with the back of the blade of a pair of scissors or the tip of a cocktail stick.

6 Cut a small wedge from each petal, working in a clockwise direction and making sure you do not remove too much paste. The size of these wedges will vary according to the overall size of the flower, but the top should measure 3–5 mm.

7 Each petal will now have to be cut in order to shape the flower. Cut the left side of the petal to a soft curve and cut the top from left to right on an angle. This means that a small triangle is cut off the top of each petal. The right hand side of these petals is about 3 mm shorter than the left.

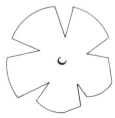

8 Press each petal between the fingers to thin and smooth the edges. Using the right hand, give the petals a forward curve while, at the same time, pressing the left side back a little.

9 Take a piece of fine or medium cotton-covered wire and form a small hook at one end. Moisten

this with a little water, then insert it into the base of the flower. Squeeze the base to secure the wire.

Calyx

Using the very tip of the scissors blades, cut five sepals at the base of the flower. These sepals can be 3–5 mm in length. Hold the flower in the left hand. Point the tip of the blades down towards the base of the flower. In making these sepals, you will be cutting five small sections from the actual flower base, but it is important not to cut these off completely. Cut into the base but allow the piece to remain attached to the flower. Set each flower aside to dry before colouring.

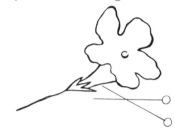

Buds

Method

1 Take a ball of paste about the size of a pea or 7–8 mm in diameter. Roll this between the fingers to form a bullet shape with slightly pointed ends.

2 Make a small hook at one end of a piece of fine or medium cotton-covered wire. Moisten and insert it into one end of the paste. Squeeze and press at the base to neaten the join. The tip of the bud can be twisted just a little to give the impression of unfurling petals. To make the calyx, cut five sepals into the base of the bud in the same way as described for the flower. Make several buds for each cluster of flowers in order to create a natural appearance.

Leaf

Method

1 Take a ball of paste which is 1 cm in diameter and roll it out thinly but leave it thicker at one end than at the other. Since leaves are often thicker than flower petals, bear this in mind when rolling out the paste. Insert the moistened, hooked end of a piece of wire into the thicker end and then pinch and squeeze to secure firmly.

2 The leaves grow in pairs along the length of the stems. Each pair is the same shape and size, although naturally they will be graded along the length of the stem. Use the drawing below to cut out several pairs of leaves varying in size. The edges are plain with no serrations.

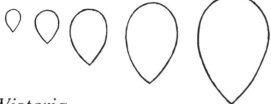

Wisteria

(see colour plate opposite p. 89)

This deciduous climber has masses of fragrant, mauve, pendulous, pea-shaped flowers in spring. The sugar replicas can also be arranged in clusters to give the same effect. No leaves are required.

Flower

Method

1 Take a ball of paste which is 8 mm in diameter and work this between the fingers to shape it into a flat wedge with a curve on the longest side. Pull the tip of this central bud with an upward motion to give it a tilt so that its base has a curve while its top has a dip close to the point. The central bud is 1.5 cm in length and 7 mm at its fattest part. Insert the moistened, hooked end of a 15 cm piece of fine cotton-covered wire into the base of the bud.

2 Make a cutter using the pattern below. Roll out a piece of paste as thinly as possible and then cut out two petals. Ball these and then attach them to either side of the bud, being sure to moisten only the base of each petal. Push the petals back a little to give them a soft outward curve.

3 Roll out another piece of paste and cut out a petal the same shape as the drawing below. Gently fold this down the centre so that a central, indented line is formed when it is reopened. Use a small balling tool or similar to work the base underside of the petal on either side of the indented line. Turn the petal over and then ball along the outer edge of

the petal. This should be done just a little in from the edge. Make sure you avoid the tip near the area of the centre line.

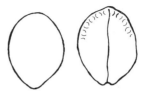

4 Moisten the base of the petal and then attach it to the base of the flower. Press and squeeze to attach it securely. Push the petal back from the flower so that it tilts backwards. Some of these flowers can have this petal bending forwards a little so that when the flowers are all assembled the cluster will have a more natural appearance.

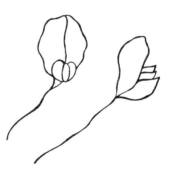

Calyx

The calyx on these flowers does not appear to have sepals. It is more like a small ball at the base of the flower.

Take a ball of paste about 3 mm in diameter. Roll it until it is completely round. Moisten the base of the flower. Insert the wire of the flower into the ball. Press and squeeze the paste against the base to ensure it is attached securely but be careful not to lose the ball-like appearance.

Buds

Follow the flower instructions to the end of step 1. You will need to make many buds in graded sizes.

Ferns

(see colour plate opposite p. 89)

There are many varieties of ferns which can be useful and attractive within a sugar flower arrangement. However, it is impossible to name and describe all the varieties which can be reproduced. The description below is a basic guide which can be adapted as required.

Method

1 Take a piece of nylon or silk-covered wire about 18–20 cm in length. Cut eight pieces of extra wire into 3–5 cm lengths, and arrange these from shortest to longest. Hold the shortest of these wires about 1.5 cm from the top of the long central wire so that it forms a cross. Twist the small piece of wire around the central one to attach it and form a short stem on either side of the longer stem. Be sure to twist this at least twice so that the wire is attached firmly and will not slip down the length of the centre wire. Attach all the other small wires to the central wire in the same way. Space the pieces so that the fern looks realistic when completed. No hooks are required at the end of these wires.

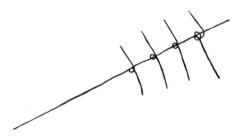

2 To add paste to the cross-wires begin at the top and complete one side and then the other of a cross-wire. Take a small ball of paste about 5 mm in diameter and roll it to a bullet shape. Insert the wire into the centre of the paste. Press and squeeze the paste so that it completely covers the wire at both ends. If the paste is actually a little longer than the wire at the tip, this will help to produce a more natural looking fern.

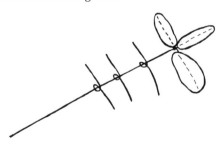

3 Trim the paste with the aid of a small pair of scissors. Each leaflet should be 2 cm in length and 6–8 mm in width with a soft, rounded curve at both ends. Make sure the paste covers the wires at the join.

4 Use the blade of a pair of scissors to indent a soft, central vein along each leaflet. Bend and curve each pair of leaflets so that they match. Continue in this way so that all pairs are alike. Space the pairs evenly along the whole stem or spike. Set aside to dry thoroughly before colouring.

Design your own special cakes from the selection of flora presented in this section. You can also combine your favourite spring flowers with your own presentation methods to produce cakes with a difference.

RECIPES

Cake Recipes

The size of a cake is determined by the amount of butter used. The following table is a guide to the size of tin required for different volumes of cake mixture according to weight of butter.

Cake mixture	Size of tin
125 g butter	15 cm
250 g butter	20 cm
500 g butter	25 cm
750 g butter	30 cm

The volume of cake mixture required for a particular fancy tin can be assessed in the following way. Fill a round or square 20 cm tin with water to within 2 cm of the top. Pour the water into a measuring jug and note the volume. Use this as a guide for future requirements. For example, a fancy tin which takes only half the volume of water held by the 20 cm tin requires half the basic recipe quantity.

Basic Fruit Cake

(½ lb butter mixture for 20 cm tin)

250 g raisins
250 g currants
125 g mixed peel
125 g glacé cherries
500 g sultanas
125 g blanched almonds, chopped
1 tablespoon glycerine
½ cup rum, brandy or sherry
250 g butter
250 g sugar
1 tablespoon marmalade
5 eggs, beaten
250 g plain flour
60 g self-raising flour
pinch salt
1 teaspoon ground nutmeg
1 teaspoon mixed, ground spice

Mix this cake with the hands to avoid damaging the fruit. The natural warmth of the body will also allow for even creaming.

Preheat oven to 180°C.

Chop the large fruits and the nuts. Place all the fruits and nuts into a bowl and then pour over the rum and glycerine and allow to stand a minimum of 24 hours. If a richer flavour is required, more of the liquor can be used and the mixture can be allowed to stand for up to a month. Stir the fruit daily and keep the bowl well-covered to avoid evaporation of the liquid.

Sift the dry ingredients together.

Cream the butter and sugar. Add the marmalade and keep working the mixture.

Gradually add in the eggs a little at a time, mixing thoroughly between each addition.

If the mixture curdles at this point add a little sifted flour after each addition of egg. This ensures that the baked cake will have the fruit evenly distributed.

Add about half of the remaining quantity of dry ingredients to the mixture and combine well. Add half the fruit and mix in thoroughly. Add the remaining flour and the last of the fruit. Stir very well and then set aside until the tin has been prepared (see p. 16).

Place the cake mixture into the tin and then drop it from a 1 metre height to release the air bubbles from the cake. Take a glass of hot water and a soup spoon. Dip the spoon into the water and smooth down the top of the cake. Repeat this until a very fine film of water has formed all over the top of the cake. Make a small depression in the centre of the cake with the spoon.

Cover the top of the tin with a piece of aluminium foil and place it on a baking tray. Lower the oven temperature to 140°C and bake the cake slowly for 3–4 hours.

When the cake is cooked remove it from the oven. Leave it in the tin with its foil covering intact. Cover it with a thick towel for 24 hours so that the steam will condense and be returned to the cake, ensuring a rich, moist fruit cake.

The following range of cakes is offered as an alternative for those who may wish to use a cake other than the traditional fruit cake. Some cakes are made from the paler dried and glacé fruits for variety and change. Unless otherwise stated, mix all the cakes in the same way as you do for the basic cake.

De Luxe Fruit Cake

60 g glacé ginger
125 g pitted dates
250 g dried or glacé pineapple
250 g dried or glacé apricots
60 g glacé orange
125 g pitted prunes
60 g dried figs
125 g glacé red cherries
125 g currants
250 g sultanas
1 cup dark rum
250 g butter
250 g raw sugar
1 tablespoon pear jam
6 eggs
200 g plain flour
60 g self-raising flour
1 teaspoon mixed, ground spice
1 teaspoon ground nutmeg

Pear and Ginger Cake

180 g glacé ginger
500 g glacé pears
500 g glacé green plums
200 g blanched almonds, chopped
½–1 cup dry vermouth
250 g butter
250 g sugar
1 tablespoon pear and ginger jam
4 eggs
200 g plain flour
60 g self-raising flour
1 teaspoon ground cinnamon

This cake is baked in the same way as the Basic Fruit Cake (see p. 95) for a period of 3–4 hours. Note that the finished cake will be pale gold in colour with golden and green fruits.

Tropical Delight Fruit Cake

500 g dried or glacé pineapple
500 g dried apricots
125 g glacé cherries
60 g glacé orange
60 g glacé peaches
60 g hazelnuts, chopped
1 cup brandy
250 g butter
250 g sugar
1 tablespoon plum and peach jam
5 eggs
200 g plain flour
60 g self-raising flour
1 cup desiccated coconut

Allow the fruit to stand in the brandy for a minimum of three days. This cake has a wonderful range of pale colours highlighted by the red of the glacé cherries. Bake for 3–4 hours.

Dark, Rich Plum Cake

750 g pitted prunes
125 g currants
375 g sultanas
125 g cherries
1 cup port
250 g butter
250 g sugar
1 tablespoon plum jam
4 eggs
250 g plain flour
60 g self-raising flour
1 teaspoon nutmeg
1 teaspoon mixed spice

This cake is very moist and dark so it may need to cook for slightly longer than the Basic Fruit Cake. Care should be taken when covering with icing because it will be very soft. Note also that this cake does not rise at all and can sometimes be very low and flat. It is a wonderful cake for those who enjoy the full, rich and mellow flavours of dark fruits. Bake for 4–5 hours.

Croquembouche

A croquembouche is made from small, filled choux pastry cases (profiteroles). It is a wonderfully impressive cake that makes a lovely change for weddings, especially since it can be served as the dessert. Once filled, the profiteroles are assembled into a tall cone and decorated at the top. They can be filled with chocolate flavoured cream or with pastry cream and then decorated either with melted chocolate or spun toffee.

Profiteroles

1 litre water
400 g unsalted butter
pinch salt
1 tablespoon sugar
500–550 g self-raising flour
6 eggs

Place the water, butter, salt and sugar in a pan and bring to the boil. Draw the pan away from the heat and then add the flour, being sure to mix well. Once the mixture is smooth, return the pan to the heat and continue stirring. The mixture needs to become smooth and draw away from the sides of the pan. When this happens, remove it from the heat and allow to cool a little.

Add the eggs one at a time, mixing very well after each addition. Pipe the mixture onto a tray making the balls uniformly 5 cm in size. Bake these at 190°C for 45–60 minutes or until they are firm and completely dry inside. Cool, then store in an airtight container until required.

Pastry Cream

This is a rich cream which makes a wonderful filling for the profiteroles.

2 litres milk
vanilla essence to taste
16 egg yolks
½ kg sugar
250 g flour

Bring the milk to the boil. Cream together the yolks, sugar and flour, then pour the milk over them in a stream while still mixing. Return the mixture to the heat for 2–5 minutes, stirring all the time. Although this can be used while the cream is still warm it is best to cool it first. Place a layer of buttered paper on the surface to avoid the cream forming a skin. Fill the puffs by piping the cream into them.

Paste Recipes

The following two recipes for pastes are very similar. The first is a basic and very reliable one while the second is an adaptation. Ingredients are the same except for the addition of tragacanth gum. The second recipe also requires the liquids to be whipped to incorporate air into the mixture.

Note that due to climatic changes many of the stronger tragacanth pastes can become very stiff and unyielding after a short time. If tragacanth gum is unavailable or too expensive, it is possible to use arabic gum in its place. This gum is obtained from the wattle tree. Arabic gum is less absorbent and tends to be more grainy so slightly more may be required. All recipes made with any gum tend to have a shorter lifespan even when stored in the freezer.

Gum Paste

1 tablespoon gelatine
1 teaspoon cream of tartar
½ cup water
500 g pure icing sugar
1 cup cornflour

Place the first three ingredients in a pan and heat for a short time to dissolve the gelatine. Do not overheat or the gelatine properties will be destroyed. Heat to blood temperature only.

Add the dry ingredients and stir well. Place a moist cloth on the mixture and allow to cool for an hour. Remove the cloth, then stir once again. Pack into small containers and store in the freezer. No thawing time is required so remove from the freezer as needed. This mixture will keep for a minimum of six months when stored in the freezer.

Whether the paste is freshly made or has been frozen, allow it to stand for 24 hours. Take small pieces of the paste and add cornflour until a nice, firm mixture has been worked up. The amount of cornflour required varies but the paste is ready when it feels like Plasticine and becomes white. When ready, place in a plastic bag to avoid drying out. If working in very hot conditions, note that the paste dries out very quickly. If your hands are too hot, cool them occasionally to reduce problems with drying. Dried out pieces of paste cannot be reused so discard them.

Note that if more elasticity is required, the gelatine quantity can be increased by up to double the amount quoted. This will make the paste very springy.

Tragacanth Gum Paste

1 tablespoon gelatine
1 teaspoon cream of tartar
1 teaspoon tragacanth gum
½ cup water
500 g pure icing sugar
1 cup cornflour

Place the first four items in a pan and heat them to blood temperature. Stir very well to ensure the gum and gelatine dissolve properly. The gum will occasionally make the liquid look speckled.

Place the mixture in the warmed mixing bowl of an electric beater or blender and turn the mixer on high or to whip. Leave this on for a minimum of 5 minutes until the liquid seems firmer and very frothy. It will also increase in volume. Add the dry ingredients gradually while still on high. When ready this mixture will be very white and light. Place in small containers and store in the freezer. When ready to use, work it in the same way as for the previous paste but note that it will require less cornflour.

Icings

Depending on the size of the cake, the amount of icing required will vary so the following chart will be of assistance.

Cake size	Icing required
15 cm	500–700 g
20 cm	1 kg
25 cm	1.5 kg
30 cm	2 kg

This chart refers only to the almond and soft icings. A little more icing will usually be required for patching any holes or cracks and either is suitable for this work.

Soft Icing

This icing is also known as sugar paste, fondant or plastic icing, according to the manufacturer. No recipes are included for this icing because it is now readily available in stores. The purchased icing is often more reliable in its consistency than the home-made product. The icing is rolled out with a rolling pin in the same way as pastry and it is used in a similar way.

Almond Icing

Again, no recipe is given because the bought icing is superior in consistency to the home-made.

Royal Icing

500 g pure icing sugar
2–3 egg whites
lemon juice if required

Depending on the work which is to be done you may or may not have to sift the icing sugar. However, if flowers are to be piped it is often not necessary to sift the icing. If fine extension work is to be done, it is necessary to sift the icing 3–4 times. Use a fine piece of silk or a very fine gauge sifter for this work. It is now possible to buy superfine, pure icing sugar. This sugar does not require sifting if used while it is fresh.

Sift the icing sugar if required. Break the egg white with a fork and then add it to the icing sugar and mix very well. Stir with a knife until the mixture looks smooth and very white. Add lemon juice as required. Place a fine film of plastic on the surface of the icing to stop a skin from forming. Note that this should be left on the icing all the time or the hard skin which forms will block the tip on fine tubes.

If a particularly fluffy and smooth icing is required, it is a good idea to whip the egg white first and then add the sugar gradually, mixing well after each addition.

Royal icing is used for piping such things as embroidery, lace, extension work and, of course, flowers and shell borders.

Royal icing will keep in the refrigerator for 2–6 weeks. It is best, however, to make up fresh batches each time. If this is not possible, draw away any dry icing from the top of the bowl and then remix it to return some body to the icing.

Soft-peak and Firm-peak Icings

The consistency of royal icing needs to be adjusted according to its use. For fine-line work the icing needs to be soft and free flowing while for flowers or shell borders it needs to be much firmer so that the shape will hold. The consistency can be varied by increasing or reducing the amount of liquid which is added to the icing sugar. If just a little extra liquid is required, it is possible to make adjustments by just adding a squeeze of lemon juice. If the mixture is very dry and will not hold together, another egg white will be required. Note that egg whites vary in size throughout the year so adjustments need to be made.

To test that royal icing is at the soft-peak stage draw the icing up to a peak with a knife. The peak should begin to collapse immediately but should not disappear altogether. Firm-peak icing will retain a stiff peak.

Paper Cones or Bags
Method

1 When using a sheet of parchmentene paper, fold and cut it according to the illustration below to produce 16 triangles.

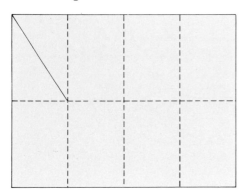

2 Take corner A of one triangle in the left hand and roll it over until it forms a straight line with B and X.

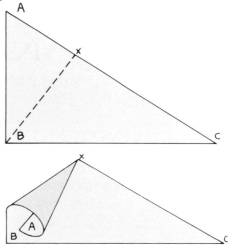

3 Take corner C and wrap it firmly around the partly formed cone. The paper should overlap a little at the outside join. All the points should meet B. They are then folded inwards twice to secure the cone. Ensure that the cone is wide enough to be able to be filled with royal icing.

4 Half fill with royal icing then fold the top of the cone inwards to provide a firm, flat area on which to rest your thumb while piping. Cut a small hole at the tip of the cone. If a tube is to be used, cut the paper 1–2 cm from the tip and drop the tube in before filling and folding the cone as described. Commence piping by pressing the top, flat area with your thumb. Support the cone with your other fingers but do not squeeze its sides otherwise it will leak and burst at the top.

Edible Gloss

60 ml water
60 g gelatine
60 g glucose

Place all the ingredients in a pan and heat gently until the gelatine has dissolved. While still warm brush onto dry items as required. This glaze may be stored in a jar in the refrigerator. Reheat before using again.

CAKE DESIGNS

Complete designs (reduced in size) are given at the top of each page. The components of the designs are repeated below in the actual size used on each cake.

Colour plate opposite p. 32.

Colour plate opposite p. 48.

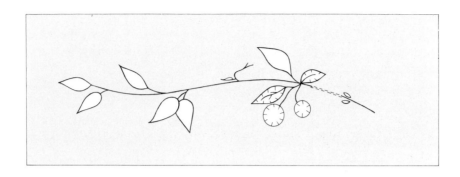

Right colour plate between pp. 48–49.

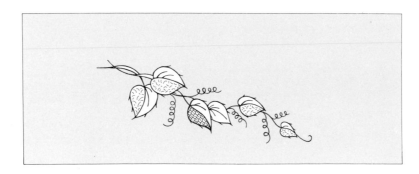

Colour plate opposite p. 49.

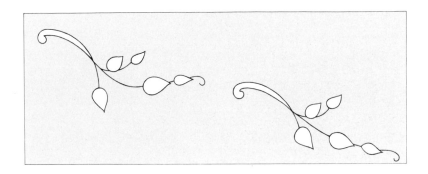

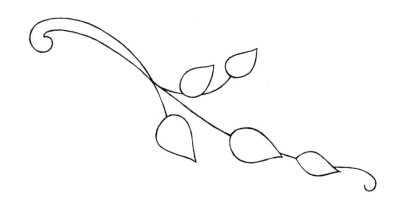

Colour plate opposite p. 80.

Colour plate opposite p. 88. Design for top tier.

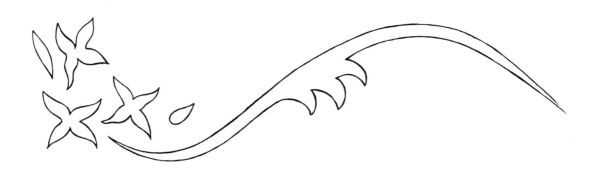

Colour plate opposite p. 88. Design for middle tier.

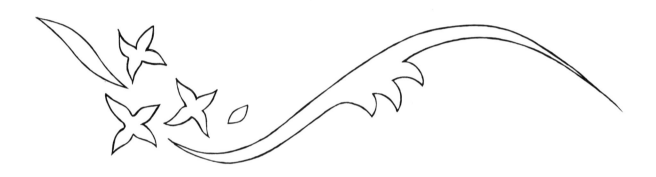

Colour plate opposite p. 88. Design for bottom tier.

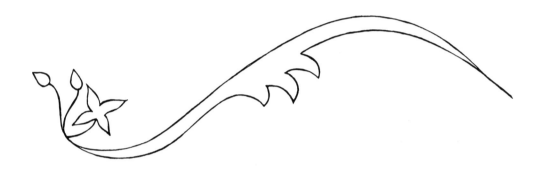

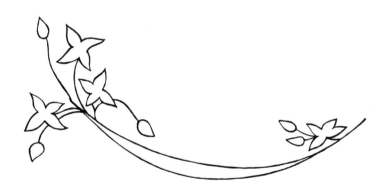

Colour plate opposite p. 89. Embroidery design for
front (above) and back (below) of top tier.

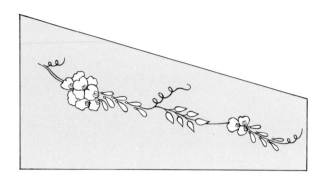

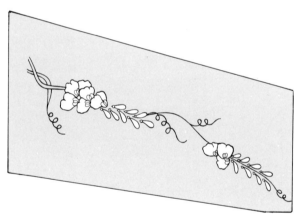

Colour plate opposite p. 89. Embroidery design for
front of bottom tier.

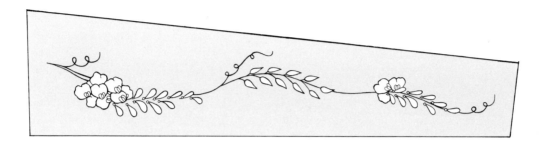

Colour plate opposite p. 89. Embroidery design for
back of bottom tier.

INDEX

Page numbers in *italics* refer to illustrations.

111